SWAMP YANKEE

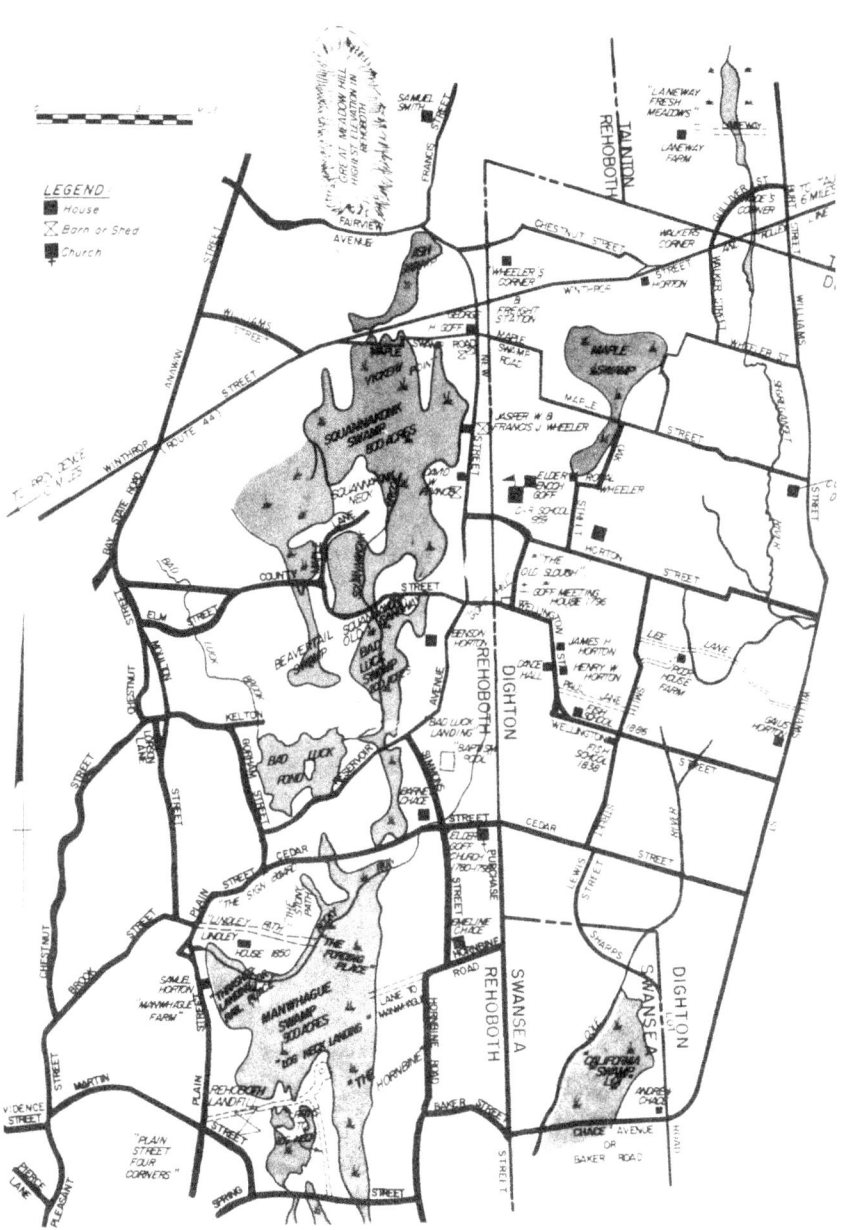

WEST DIGHTON AND EAST REHOBOTH NEIGHBORHOOD
circa 1880 – 1910

SWAMP YANKEE

BY
E. OTIS DYER

A local history of farm life and wood cutting in the swamps and woodlands in the Dighton-Rehoboth, Massachusetts area, circa 1900

WIPF & STOCK · Eugene, Oregon

Resource Publications
A division of Wipf and Stock Publishers
199 W 8th Ave, Suite 3
Eugene, OR 97401

Swamp Yankee
By Dyer, E. Otis
Copyright©1994 by Dyer, E. Otis
ISBN 13: 978-1-5326-5103-8
Publication date 2/14/2018
Previously published by William S. Sullwold, Publishing, 1994

INTRODUCTION

My interest in the life of Roy W. Horton as a typical Swamp Yankee and my desire to explore local history at the turn of the twentieth century began with an ordinary surveying assignment which I never expected to lead me beyond the site in question. In 1958 I was asked to survey the site of the proposed Dighton-Rehoboth Regional High School on the boundary line of the two towns.

My project was not only to survey the perimeter and topography of this area but also to find out who owned the various parcels within the locus and to plot them on a land taking plan. Because there were no assessor maps at that time for guidance, extensive and detailed deed research in the Registry of Deeds in Taunton, Massachusetts was required. I had to trace many vague deeds back to the early 1800's to find a suitable description before I could make any sense out of them. In these old deeds I came across the names of earlier land owners: Andrew Goff, Emerson Goff, David W. Francis, Royal Wheeler, and Benjamin Goff. I also determined that around 1800 the whole area had belonged to Elder Enoch Goff and had been occupied by him as his homestead farm up to the time of his death in 1810.

While surveying the site, I noted that the land was covered with brush and woods and laced with stone walls enclosing many irregularly shaped lots. Old cart paths and lanes covered with growth were still distinguishable on the ground. Occasionally I found pieces of barbed wire of a variety no longer being manufactured drooping off tottering cedar fence posts or hanging out from near the center of large trees. Lots with a good quality of soil and few rocks, often covered with large white pines and sprinkled with red cedar, contrasted with more swampy or rocky marginal lots under a heavy growth of hard wood. These distinguishing landscape features indicated to me that much of the land at various times had been used to pasture cattle and raise crops. The white pine and red cedar, always the first trees to appear on abandoned farm land, meant that these lots had been tilled at a more recent date. The stone walls found within the hardwood forest indicated that someone had once attempted to farm even that land at an earlier time. The oak, ash, and maple trees found on the more marginal lands, having long ago crowded out the pine and cedar, proved that these lots had not been tilled or pastured for perhaps over 100 years. As a part time farmer with an interest in local history, I was curious to know more about the people who had once lived in the neighborhood and attempted to farm this land; I never expected to satisfy that curiosity.

After following the chain of title from these early land owners to the present in the Registry of Deeds, I found that many of the lots had been carved out of the original Elder Enoch Goff farm and that, after his wife's death in 1816, they had been passed from one person to another until Henry Wheaton Horton purchased many of them in 1919. Mr. Horton having died some years ago, the owners in 1958 were Roy W. Horton, Henry's son, and Elsie, Roy's wife. Since I had some trouble locating the modern owners of some of the other lots, I decided to turn to Roy for help. Therefore, one day I visited Roy Horton at his home on Wellington Street in Dighton. Roy was then in his late fifties and living on the farm which his grandfather James H. Horton (1837-1907) once owned. This farm bordered on the dairy farm where Roy had been born in 1899 and brought up during the first decades of this century. Roy's father, Henry Wheaton Horton, had died in 1943 and at the time of my visit this dairy was being operated by Roy's brother Raymond (1895-1965) and Raymond's son Harlan (1929-1991). Roy dabbled in various farming activities, but his main occupation was carpentry and he had become a successful house builder.

In that visit Roy answered my specific questions about the Regional High School site and went further to begin the first of many fascinating conversations that I was to enjoy off and on over the next thirty years.

I was impressed by Roy's exceptional memory of past events and of the old timers of his boyhood. Both his father and grandfather had had a similar interest in local history and often had told Roy about life in their earlier years as well as anecdotes about people, or as Roy would say, "characters" they once knew. Roy remarked that the Hortons were always interested in local history and people. Roy knew not only the relationships of all the old families in the neighborhood including those of his own family, but he could often add something interesting about their experiences and personalities. These recollections of three generations have offered me a unique record of what life was like for over a 120 year period in West Dighton and East Rehoboth.

It was a much simpler life then: the economy was almost wholly dependent on farming and harvesting the woodlands and swamp land for lumber, cordwood, and other forest products, and the main sources of power were the horse and the ox. Roy's boyhood spanned this time when farming was still being extensively carried on in West Dighton, using many of these old ways carried over from the eighteenth century. As Roy grew older, however, these old farming practices were gradually being abandoned because of the introduction of mechanically powered farm machinery, the almost universal ownership of the automobile, and the use of coal or fuel oil and kerosene for heat and cooking. At first the more marginal lands were let go into brush and woods, as I had observed at the school site, and more recently many have been converted into house lot subdivisions. On the old Horton farm on Wellington Street the Peach Orchard, the Grintry lot, the Hathaway lot, and other tracts now lie within a housing project serviced by Fieldstone Drive. Where Roy, his father, and brothers once tilled the soil, raised the land, cut hay, and harvested crops, there are now lawns, and the only crops grown are in a few backyard gardens.

As I became more closely acquainted with Roy and as I listened to more of his stories, I began to realize that I had a rare opportunity to learn about local life in a much earlier era. Believing these recollections to be of historical interest to future generations, I began to take notes on what Roy said. When I told Roy about my plan someday to write a book based on his boyhood farm experiences, he encouraged me to do so and volunteered to help in any way he could. Unfortunately, because of business commitments, several years slipped by before I could begin the work; by then Roy had died during his 90th year. As I finally began to write this book I soon found the need to interview other persons familiar with the Hortons in order to gain information to fill in missing details, particularly on life on the Horton farm in later years. Roy's family, relatives, and friends supplied this material and added also their own anecdotes about life on their own family farms in West Dighton and easterly Rehoboth at the beginning of this century.

I had noticed when I consulted the *HISTORY OF REHOBOTH* by the Rev. George H. Tilton (1917) and the *HISTORY OF DIGHTON* by Helen Lane (1962) that little reference was made to the history of these portions of both towns. In Tilton's *History* there are over 200 biographical sketches of prominent Rehoboth families who lived during the nineteenth and early twentieth century, but not one of the very successful farmers along the New Street section of Rehoboth was mentioned. Perhaps this omission is because the book was written by the local Congregational minister who being church oriented emphasized primarily people and events affiliated with that church and with the other numerous religious denominations in various parts of Rehoboth. Since most of the residents in this part of Rehoboth attended the Goff Church (the present West Dighton Christian Church) at the corner of Horton and Wellington Streets in West Dighton, the farmers of this neighborhood may have been recorded to be chiefly under the influence of West Dighton and of little importance to Rehoboth. Similarly in Lane's Dighton *History* there is little reference to the people of West Dighton; evidently they were not considered significant in that town's development. Moreover, on the historical map included in the book only a couple of house locations are shown in the west part of Dighton. This omission, however, is not due to any religious orientation, but because the center of Dighton interest has always been along the Taunton River on the opposite side of the town, the commercial section of Dighton. Indeed, the West Dighton and East Rehoboth areas seemed to be sort of a no-man's land in local history. Because I had now developed a curiosity about these sections of the two towns, whetted by additional information given to me by Roy's relatives and neighbors, I decided to expand this book to include the new material and to try to fill in some of this gap in local history.

Before I had ever met Roy Horton back in 1959, I had occasionally heard the expression *Swamp Yankee* apparently used to describe an individual native to Rehoboth or Dighton and of Yankee heritage. In fact, I had a few times been called that name myself without knowing really what it meant. I have even noted recently that Governor William Weld of Massachusetts was called a swamp yankee by a *BOSTON GLOBE* reporter in a manner considered complimentary. The precise meaning of the term and its exact origin are, however, ambiguous and even controversial, and still subjects for continuing research.

Today in this region swamp yankee is generally held to refer to a descendant of an early immigrant Anglo-Saxon family who is notably self-reliant, industrious, honest, and trustworthy. Although originating in the nineteenth century, the term is still today well known and commonly used in the area running from the southeast corner of Connecticut, up the seacoast through South County in Rhode Island, into southeastern Massachusetts, and stopping abruptly at Cape Cod, all regions noted for a multitude of swamps as well as Yankees. Aside from an occasional reference to the name in Massachusetts, north of Danvers and west to Pittsfield—out of the range of extensive swamps—the term is evidently unknown. The conclusion that a swamp yankee lives and works around swamps can be drawn with some certainty and will be accepted in that sense in this book. For my purpose, then, a swamp yankee will refer to an individual of British ancestry who possesses the traditional yankee virtues of thrift, industry, honesty, reliability, and independence and lives near and makes at least part of his living from swamps, by what Roy called "swamping." (See Appendix II)

My long friendship and countless conversations with Roy Horton have led me to designate him as truly representative of a swamp yankee, and as such he will appear in this book. Roy, however, is not alone; other local swamp yankees who will come into this book include Enoch Goff (not a swamp worker but a swamp frequenter, and certainly a prototypical yankee); Henry W. Horton and his sons Raymond and Elwood Horton and grandson Harlan Horton; David W. Francis and his son Frederick E. Francis; Jasper Wheeler and his son Francis J. Wheeler and grandsons Eddie and Henry Wheeler; George H. Goff and his son Arthur H. Goff; and Samuel Smith and his sons Samuel, Bryon, Elisha, Horace, and John.

From my initial survey of the Dighton-Rehoboth Regional High School site the scope of my work has steadily widened through extensive research and interviews with Roy and others, and finally has evolved from the intended simple biography of Roy Horton to embrace also a description of farm life and practices in turn-of-the-twentieth century Rehoboth and Dighton and a re-creation of the days when swamping dominated the Rehoboth economy. However, the focus of my book remains Roy Horton, farmer and swamp yankee, whose recollections form its base and whose life is its inspiration.

ACKNOWLEDGEMENTS

Although the chief sources of this book are the conversations I held with Roy W. Horton over a number of years, I have incorporated into the book a number of additional stories and anecdotes given to me by several other individuals, some of Roy's generation, about their experiences on their families' West Dighton or Rehoboth farms during the first decades of this century. I owe many thanks to these contributors for their assistance and time.

Pearl Wheeler Quint has kindly shared with me her memories of life on the farm during the early 1900's. As a young girl she was sent to live on the farm of her grandfather, Francis J. Wheeler. During this time the Wheelers were still making charcoal on the farm, cutting cordwood in the swamps, raising strawberries, and supplying the nearby city markets with these and other farm products.

Norma Wheeler Blackledge had fortunately interviewed her father Francis E. Wheeler (1902-1986) before his death about his boyhood memories of the same Wheeler farm. She generously passed on to me her notes on that conversation, and also lent several old family farm photos.

I am grateful to Horace Smith (1909-1992) for offering his recollections of the hard life which he, his parents, and brothers led, trying to eke out a living on their Francis Street, Rehoboth farm by tending a dairy herd and cutting thousands of cords of wood and railroad ties on the slopes of Great Meadow Hill for the Pawtucket-Attleboro firewood market and street railway company during the first decades of this century. His daughter Carol Entwistle kindly let me use several family photographs.

Harlan Horton (1929-1991), a couple of weeks before his death, spent several hours with me describing the Horton farm activities during its later years when it was being operated by him and his father, Raymond Horton. Both he and Roy's son-in-law, Francis J. McClellan, the hired man on the farm at the time of the fire, were especially helpful in supplying information on that catastrophe. Francis' wife Janice McClellan, along with Priscilla Chase and Carol Kingman, Roy's other two daughters, kindly let me borrow family pictures of the Horton family.

I thank also Elaine Varley of the Dighton Historical Society who searched the Society's archives and found a number of old house photos of the Dighton area that she let me borrow.

Evelyn Holden Elting, who was brought up on the Marble Dairy Farm, Williams Street, Dighton, had many memories of the Taunton door to door dairy business her family conducted and loaned to me a number of excellent pictures of this dairy enterprise, all very helpful.

Others who offered their assistance whom I wish to thank are Talbot Tweedy, Esq. of Taunton who as a boy spent his summers on the Tinkham Farm, Smith Street, Dighton; Miriam Johnson of Attleboro who visited her grandparents at the Arthur H. Goff farm on New Street, Rehoboth; Betsey Dyer Obar for her original poems about Roy and swamps and for proof reading the manuscript; Larry Carswell and E. Otis Dyer, Jr. for also proof reading; the *TAUNTON DAILY GAZETTE* for letting me borrow pictures of Roy from their files; Suzanne Withers and Diane Alba both of Rehoboth for the informative articles they wrote about Roy when they were correspondents for the *TAUNTON DAILY GAZETTE* and *ATTLEBORO SUN;* Ernest L. Horton of Dighton who was born on a farm on the shores of Squannakonk Swamp and as a boy moved to the farm on Wellington Street, Dighton, where he still lives, for his comments on farming during the first decades of this century; and John McPherson, the minister of the West Dighton Christian Church (Elder Goff's Meeting House); Bethany Gaulin Carroll, Nancy Cutts and Lydia D. Carswell for drawing the maps; Bethany Gaulin Carroll and Dorothy McNally for typing the manuscript; Paula M. Muggleton for setting the type; and Joseph Carpenter, Jr. for his drawings of the Horton farm and oxen; and Richard Benjamin for photographs.

I also wish to thank Pamela Holmes of Kent, Great Britain for allowing me to use her poem *The Cow;* Ann Roper of Northants, Great Britain for allowing me to use her drawing of a boy driving a cow; and Christopher Hall, Editor of the Countryman Magazine, published in Burford, Great Britain, for giving me permission to use the poem and drawing which had appeared in the summer of 1992 edition of that magazine.

Lastly, I wish to thank my sister Justine Dyer Phillips of Falmouth, Massachusetts, for the many hours she spent offering suggestions and editing the manuscript.

TABLE OF CONTENTS

Introduction		i
Acknowledgements		vii
List of Illustrations and Photographs		xi
List of Maps and Charts		xiii
List of Poems		xiv
Part I ROY W. HORTON, FARMER		1
Chapter I	The Paul Farm	3
Chapter II	The Horton Farm	13
Chapter III	Farming in the Early 1900's	19
Chapter IV	Farm Animals	53
Chapter V	Schools	61
Chapter VI	Friends, Neighbors, Characters	65
Chapter VII	Later Years	73
Part II ROY W. HORTON, SWAMPER		81
Chapter I	Swamps	83
Chapter II	Swamping	89
Chapter III	Woodlots	101
Chapter IV	Elder Enoch Goff	105
Chapter V	Wood Operators	115
Part III IMPRESSIONS AND REFLECTIONS		155
Chapter I	The Neighborhood Today	157
Chapter II	The Swamps Today	159
Chapter III	Great Meadow Hill Today	165
Chapter IV	Roy W. Horton, Swamp Yankee	175
Appendix I	Roy W. Horton Eulogy by Frank Coughlan	183
Appendix II	The Meaning of the Term "Swamp Yankee"	187
Appendix III	Additional Dairy Economics	189
Appendix IV	List of Henry W. Horton Farms and Woodlots in 1943	190
Appendix V	List of George Hathaway Goff Property in 1903	192
Appendix VI	List of David W. Francis Property in 1913	194
Appendix VII	List of Francis J. Wheeler Property in 1928	197
Bibliography		199
Notes		200
Index		207
About the Author		217

LIST OF ILLUSTRATIONS AND PHOTOGRAPHS

Roy W. Horton "Swamp Yankee"	2
James H. Horton House, West Dighton in 1896	9
James H. Horton Barn, West Dighton	10
Henry Wheaton Horton House and Barn, West Dighton, circa 1900 and at present	14
Hardware Stores, Taunton, Ma. circa 1900	16
Marble Dairy Co. Sign	18
Marble Dairy Wagons in 1912	21
The C.C. Marble Dairy, Dighton circa 1910 and at present	23
Cows grazing in front yard circa 1896	28
Perryville Grist Mill, Rehoboth circa 1910 and present site	38
Dam at Perryville Pond, Rehoboth	39
Exterior and Interior of the Horton Barn in West Dighton	45
Interior of the Horton Barn	46
The Hall of Office, West Dighton	50
The Cow by Ann Roper	52
The Horton Family Working with their oxen	56
Shoeing Oxen	58
Former Fish School, West Dighton	60
The Richard K. Witerell House, West Dighton, circa 1900 and at present	64
Anawan Inn, Rehoboth and site today	72
The Horton Barn Fire, West Dighton in 1964	79
Fred M. Smith Hauling Cedar Logs	82
Henry W. Horton and Ox Cart	97
"Over at Shubes" present Dighton-Rehoboth School	104
Elder Goff's Meeting House Goff Hill, West Dighton	107
Shubael Goff - Angela Bilodeau House, Rehoboth	108
Enoch Goff's Baptismal Pool	112
The David W. Francis House, Rehoboth	114
Views of the Francis J. Wheeler House, Rehoboth	126
Pictures of the Wheeler Family, Rehoboth	128

Edward F., Elkanah and Henry Walker
 Wheeler, circa 1887 129
The Henry W. Wheeler House, Rehoboth 132
The Francis J. Wheeler corn sheller 133
The George Hathaway Goff House, Rehoboth
 circa 1910 and at present 136
The exterior and interior of the George
 Hathaway Goff barn, Rehoboth 138
The Taunton Teaming Company Advertisement 140
The Wagon Shed at the George Hathaway
 Goff Farm, Rehoboth 141
Samuel Smith as a Horse Car Conductor 148
The Smith Boys, circa 1918 149
Horace Smith stacking firewood 154
Recent view, Horton Barn, West Dighton 156
Moe Horton and his barn and house, Rehoboth 164
Rehoboth Fire Tower and present view of the National
 Guard Building, Great Meadow Hill, Rehoboth 167
H.P. Lovecraft fireplace, Great Meadow
 Hill, Rehoboth 173
Roy W. Horton Logging Sled 179

LIST OF MAPS AND CHARTS

West Dighton and East Rehoboth Neighborhood
 circa 1900 .... Inside cover
The Paul - Horton Farm circa 1900 4
The Horton and Paul Family Genealogical Chart 6
Farm Buildings at the Paul - Horton Farm
 in West Dighton, circa 1900 47
Swamps and Landings in Rehoboth circa 1900 80
Former Elder Enoch Goff Farm and the
 D. W. Francis Lots in Dighton and Rehoboth 106
Location of the Elder Enoch Goff's
 First Church and Baptismal Pool 110
Detail Plan of the Elder Goff Baptismal Pool in Rehoboth 111
Genealogical Chart of the Horton - Goff Lineage 113
The Francis J. Wheeler Farm Rehoboth, circa 1910 124
Great Meadow Hill, Rehoboth, circa 1900 144

LIST OF POEMS

Roy Horton, Farm Boy, by Betsey Dexter Dyer 43
The Cow, by Pamela Holmes 52
Squannakonk Swamp, by Betsey Dexter Dyer 99
Lost on Great Meadow Hill, by Betsey Dexter Dyer 168

PART 1

ROY W. HORTON, FARMER

The farm, the farm is the right school. The reason of my deep respect for the farmer is that he is a realist, and not a dictionary. The farm is a piece of the world, the schoolhouse is not. Ralph Waldo Emerson

ROY WHEATON HORTON 1899 - 1989
"Swamp Yankee"
with Scout

Chapter I

THE PAUL FARM 1750 – 1870

By 1959, when I first met Roy, the Horton name had been well established along the westerly end of Wellington Street for over a century. Roy, however, often pointed out that although people think the Hortons lived on this land from the earliest days of the founding of Dighton, that is not true; before the Hortons lived here, the Paul* family dominated the area for the previous 100 years.

Old records in the Registry of Deeds indicate that James and Sarah Paul were living here in the eighteenth century. In 1789, approaching old age, they gave their son Peter White Paul (1760-1811) their small farm along with their cow, a heifer, a horse, two hogs, two sheep, all their household goods, and "one black boy's time." Peter now had a farm but, in return, the parents retained the right to live in the house with Peter and his family for the rest of their lives, a common arrangement in the days before the welfare and retirement systems of the twentieth century. The original Paul farm house, no longer standing, was at that time across Wellington Street from the present Horton farm house.

Peter W. Paul and his family prospered on the farm. Peter had two wives and many children. In 1816, a few years after his death, the farm was divided up among his children and widow. From his two marriages, Peter had mostly boys: Peter, James, John, Job, and Caleb. One of these sons, James Paul (1791-

---

*During the eighteenth and nineteenth centuries the Paul family name was spelled both Paul or Paull. Since the Paul version is the most frequently found on their family tombstones in the West Dighton cemetery, it will be used here.

3

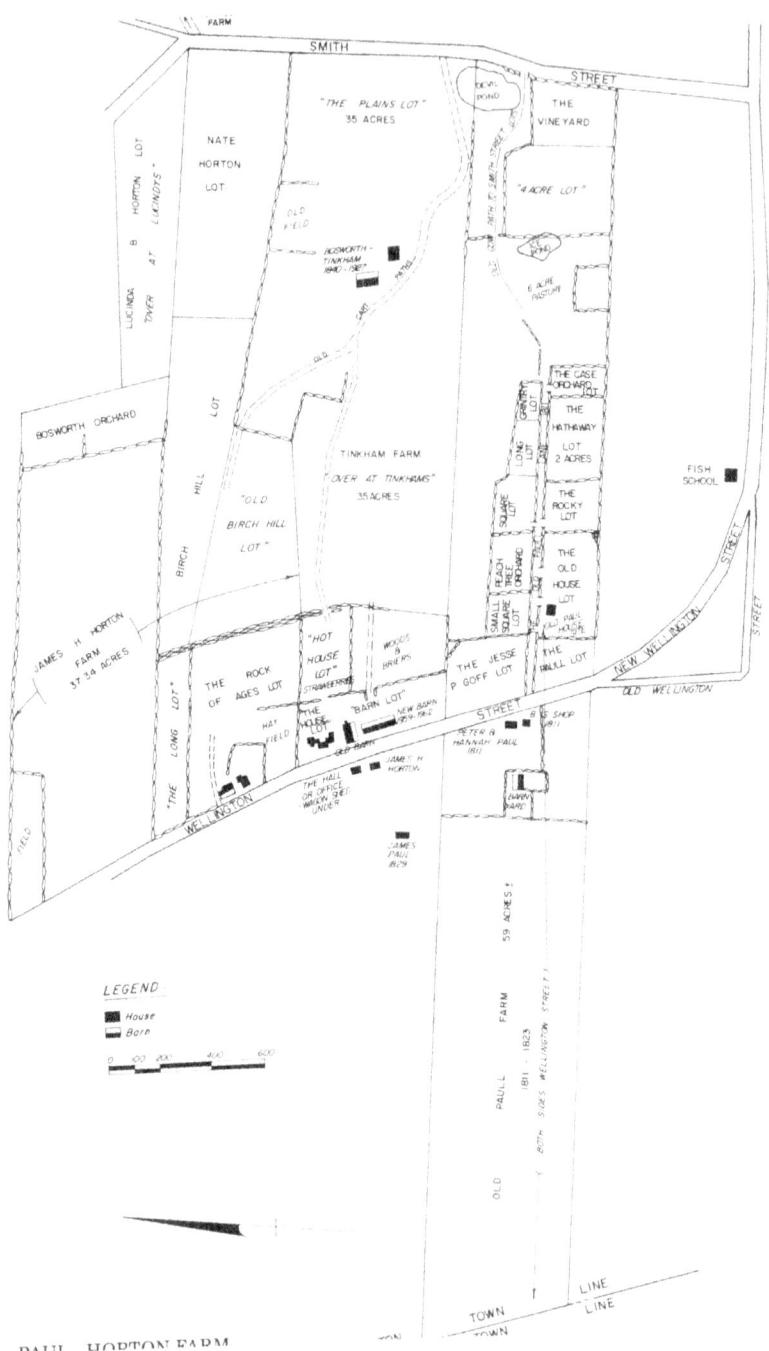

PAUL HORTON FARM

1859), purchased many of the division lots from the other heirs and reassembled much of the old farm into its original form. When James died in 1859 the farm was passed on to his son James Wheaton Paul (1814-1873), sometimes called Wheaton Paul. Roy noted it was about 1849, ten years before James' death, when his grandfather James H. Horton, age 12, appeared on the scene.

Roy's grandfather, James H. Horton (1837-1907), was born to Benson and Pamela (Briggs) Horton in Rehoboth just over the Dighton line. Pamela (1798-1861) was sometimes called Permilla. Old records indicate that Benson was descended from an old Rehoboth family that had lived in the Long Hill area of Reservoir Avenue for several generations. Benson Horton (1798-1875) was one of seven children born to Wheeler Horton (1766-1857) and Lucretia Horton (1770-1855). In the early 1800's Wheeler's father, Barnet (Barnard) Horton, conveyed to his son Wheeler his thirty acre farm on the west side of Reservoir Avenue about opposite where the present fire tower is situated. Although Barnet had conveyed the whole farm to his son, Barnet kept a half interest in the house and continued to share those quarters with his son's family.

Wheeler was not particularly prosperous and when he died in 1857 he was in rather heavy debt; his total assets, which included his house, farm, and a few personal possessions were valued at about $820.00. Since the bills owed were almost equal to these assets, his estate was almost insolvent. In later years, it was noted that the eleven children Benson and Pamela had brought up here on the Horton farm were still hale and hearty when the youngest was fifty years old, an unusual record considering the mortality rate of that era.

Roy talked little about his great grandparents Benson and Pamela Horton, but when he did, it was mostly to describe how poor they were. The two decades or so before and after the Civil War were not prosperous times for the citizens of Rehoboth and Dighton. Many small farms like those Wheeler and Benson Horton had inherited were economically unable to support a large family. Manufactured goods were becoming common even in the rural areas, and the ancient home subsistence type industries like spinning, weaving, and cobbling were being abandoned in favor of purchasing articles of food and clothing in

PARTIAL GENEALOGICAL CHART OF THE HORTON AND PAUL FAMILIES IN DIGHTON AND REHOBOTH

	PAUL FAMILY OF DIGHTON			HORTON FAMILY OF REHOBOTH	
(1)	James Paul b. 1725 d. ?	m.	Sarah White b. 1729 d. ?	Barnard (Barnet) Horton b. 1744 d. 1834 m.	Mehitabel Cole b. 1747 d.
(2)	Peter White Paul b. 1760 d. 1811	m.	Silence Briggs (second wife) b. 1765 d. 1796	Wheeler Horton b. 1766 d. 1857 m.	Lucretia Lindley b. 1770 d. 1855
(3)	James Paull b. 1791 d. 1859	m.	Betsey Paull b. 1790 d. 1874	Benson Horton b. 1798 d. 1875 m.	Permilla Briggs (Pamela) b. 1798 d. 1861
(4)	James Wheaton Paul b. 1814 d. 1873	m.	Eleanor Goff b. 1815 d. 1867	James Harlan Horton b. 1843 d. 1907	
(5)	Mary Asneth Paul b. 1843 d. 1915	m.			
(6)	Mary E. Horton b. 1861 d. 1861	Henry Wheaton Horton b. 1864 d. 1943	Hannah J. Leonard b. 1866 d. 1942	Gaius Everett Horton b. 1867 d. 1950	Nellie L. (Horton) Pierce b. 1861 d.	Lena May Horton b. 1877 d. 1943
(7)	James Harlan Horton b. 1891 d. 1910	Elwood Horton b. 1893 d. 1969	Raymond Horton b. 1895 d. 1965	George Russell Horton b. 1898 d. 1969	Roy Wheaton Horton b. 1899 d. 1989	

stores. Bartering these goods for farm produce, the way business had been conducted since the two towns had been settled, was no longer possible, and the cash needed to purchase necessities was not readily available to the country people. Almost the only source of cash was from the sale of vegetables and firewood in the Providence and Pawtucket market. Transportation was slow and tedious and only a few enterprising farms were able to purchase the necessary horse drawn equipment and tailor their farm operations to take advantage of this expanding market.

Having been raised under these economic conditions, Roy's grandfather, James H. Horton, as a youth was sent over to Wellington Street in Dighton by his parents to live with the Paul family. Roy had conflicting stories as to why this move came about. The version he most often gave was that Benson and Pamela were too poor to support young James, so they sent him at age 12 over to the Pauls' farm under some sort of an apprenticeship arrangement. This meant young James was given room, board, and clothing by the Pauls in return for laboring on their farm. The other version Roy gave was that because Benson and Pamela had five sons and the Pauls and several of their neighboring Dighton families, all named Briggs, had no sons, one by one as the sons of Benson Horton became old enough, they sought jobs on these Dighton farms. According to this second version it was not until about 1858 at age 21 that James went to work on the Paul farm as a hired man. James' four brothers, Charles, Oren, Jarvis, and Andrew, soon followed suit and lived and worked on the various "son-less" Briggs' farms in West Dighton. Roy recalled that they naturally stayed on to manage and later as soon as each of the Horton sons could save enough money, he would purchase the farm where he worked.

Roy sometimes chuckled when he recalled how his grandfather eventually became the owner of the Paul farm, not by buying it, but by getting in "by way of the back door" by marrying the Pauls' only daughter Mary. At the time of the marriage James was 22 years old and his new wife, Mary Asenth Paul (1843-1915), was age 17. The marriage was to last 48 years until James' death in 1907. Somehow James learned from the Pauls more than just how to do farm work, because as an adult he became a successful stone and brick mason and a shrewd business man. Perhaps the Pauls taught him the mason's trade or assisted him in learning it because in 1871 at age 32, while he continued to live on the Paul farm, James advertised himself as a brick and stone mason as well as a farmer. As a successful mason and farmer, he often had extra money to lend to his neighbors in return for notes and mortgages. Throughout his adult life he held mortgages on a number of properties in the area and at the time of his death at age 70 in 1907 he was still active in making loans; he had almost ten thousand dollars lent out to his neighbors, a large sum of money for those times.

Newly married, James and Mary continued to live on the Paul farm and with their in-laws shared the farm house that still stands today on Wellington Street. As the following children were born to James and Mary, conditions became understandably crowded in the Paul house: Mary E. Horton (1860-1860) who died as an infant, Nellie L. Horton (1861- ?), Henry Wheaton Horton (1864-1943) who was Roy's father, Gaius E. Horton (1867-1950), and Lena May Horton (1877-1943). Roy was told that as his grandparents' family grew, his grandfather was not getting along too well with his in-laws under these crowded conditions. To alleviate this problem James and Mary moved to a new house they built across the street from the Paul farmhouse. This is now the home of Thomas Horton, a grandson of Raymond Horton, Roy's brother.

James and Mary were to make one more move during their life time when in 1890 they bought the Henry M. Westcott homestead on Wellington Street from the Westcott heirs. The Westcott house had originally been built by Charles Goff in 1854 from a lot cut out of the old Paul farm. This is where Roy and Elsie were living when I first met them in 1959, but the house that is presently situated on the property is not the original Westcott house. The first house burned down during a chimney fire when owned by James Horton. The replacement house met a similar fate during the winter of 1893 while Lena, daughter of James and Mary, was at home. To build the present house, the Hortons immediately after the fire began cutting needed timber in the woods towards Smith Street. When the house was erected during the summer, the oak framing was still green, and to this

The third James H. Horton house on this site as it looked in 1896 on Wellington Street, West Dighton. Lena Horton, a daughter, holds the bicycle and Hannah J. Horton, mother of Roy stands beside her.

The same view today. This is supposedly the third house that has stood at this site since the first was built by Charles Goff in 1854. The first two houses burned to the ground from chimney fires.

day gives the present owners, Arthur and Jane Morton, difficulties with the uneven floors and walls. By Thanksgiving of that year the house was complete and James and his family moved in.

James H. Horton, like the other more successful farmers in the West Dighton and easterly Rehoboth area, besides furnishing most of the family's food and all of its fuel, raised a variety of extra products to sell in the nearby markets as a source of cash. The Hortons' main farming activity centered around managing a small herd of cows whose surplus milk was sold. Additional income was obtained by cutting and selling fire wood and timber and by raising a variety of vegetables for sale in the Providence market. Tomatoes, celery, potatoes, and strawberries were popular crops grown on the farm. It was noted in a newspaper report in November, 1881, that "Mr. Horton had become one of the most successful farmers in West Dighton and that he had just harvested a large quantity of celery he had grown on three-quarters of an acre." According to Roy, this celery crop most likely would have been raised on the Grintry lot on Paul Lane where the loam was black, moist, and deep.

James H. Horton Barn, Wellington Street, West Dighton

As dairy herds became more and more important for farm prosperity, cows began to receive better care and more attention was paid to raising improved breeds. James told Roy's father that at about the time of the Civil War, when he was young, cows were kept very poorly. Every farm had one or two cows for its own use, small black ones, nothing like the big Holsteins that were available in the early 1900's. During the earlier times, the feed available was so poor that most of the cows dried up (stopped giving milk) during the winter. However, during the late spring and early summer, there was always a surplus of milk because the cows thrived on the new green grass. The extra milk was made into butter and stored in the cellar for later family use or sale.

During the decades following the Civil War, the surrounding towns and cities developed rapidly into a manufacturing economy, and many of the farms if they were large enough, like the Paul - Horton farm, began to place more and more emphasis on dairy farming. The extra milk produced was sent to distributors who each day delivered it to homes in the new urban areas. The farm still supplied the owners with much of their own food and fuel, but the dairy gave them a steady source of cash to purchase manufactured goods and specialized items. Roy's father Henry and his Uncle Gaius successfully made this major conversion into dairying, each on his own farm. By the time Roy was born in the old Paul house on Wellington Street on December 8, 1899, the Pauls were dead and James H. and Mary A. Horton had a few years earlier in 1896 conveyed the Paul farm to Roy's father Henry W. Horton. The farm at that time consisted of the farmhouse, barn, outbuildings, and the "hall" across the street on 35 acres. A year before that sale, Gaius E. Horton, Henry's brother, had moved away from the homestead to his newly purchased "Old Edson Place" on both sides of Williams Street, Dighton, which consisted of a house, farm buildings, and about 60 acres of land.

The Pauls and the Hortons between them had by now occupied the Wellington Street land for over 150 years. Through many years of hard work, fields had been cleared of brush and trees, stumps removed, and the borders fenced with stone walls and fences. Some marginal lots were left in woodland, but swampland which was not then considered waste land had been cleared of the brush and trees and developed into fresh meadow hayland. Orchards with various types of fruit trees were set out. Some lots were set aside for mowing hay and others for pastures or cultivated crops. A prosperous farm had been established. Activity centered around the dairy enterprises. During the summer and fall hay and corn were harvested and brought into the barn or stacked in the yard. During the winter they were fed to the cows and from the manure produced, the fields were fertilized for a new crop to begin a new cycle. During the winter months wood cutting and swamping started in order to obtain next year's fuel supply or to earn extra cash by selling firewood timber in the market. The whole family income was dependent on crops raised on the farm and the sale of wood from their wood lots.

Chapter II

HORTON FARM
(1870-1964)

On May 28, 1890, Henry W. Horton married Hannah J. Leonard (1866-1942) of Brockton, Massachusetts, and together they began their married life in the old Paul homestead. Over the next nine years five children were born there, all boys: James Harlan Horton (1891-1910), Elwood Horton (1893-1969), Raymond A. Horton (1895-1965), George Russell Horton (1898-1969), and Roy Wheaton Horton (1899-1989). After Henry acquired the Paul-Horton farm in 1896, he operated it as a general farm, raising various crops and dealing in fire wood, but he also continued the trend begun by his father by emphasizing dairying. After Henry's parents James H. and Mary A. Horton had turned the Paul farm over to him, they continued to live next door on the old Westcott place where James continued to do a little farming on his own by raising some livestock in addition to assisting his son with farm work when able. By the time James died in 1907, Henry had begun to rely on his growing sons to help with the farm work, with the exception of Harlan who was sickly. Roy was only eight, but his second oldest brother Elwood was now fourteen; next came Raymond, age twelve, and brother Russell, age nine. Elwood and Raymond rapidly took to farming and working in the woods, their vocations for the rest of their lives. Russell was less interested in such work and preferred indoor office type employment. He attended business school and as an adult became a banker at the Industrial National (now Fleet) Bank in Providence and a Dighton Selectman. Also, to help out with the farm work was John, later known as "old John," who for many years was the trusted hired man. Roy too loved the farm, but his favorite ac-

The Henry Wheaton Horton Farmhouse and Barn circa 1900. Note the ten quart milk cans drying by the shed door. The shed, used to house wagons and cider barrels in the cellar, has since been demolished.

The same view today.

tivity was working in the woods and swamps during the winter months.

Roy had a lifetime admiration for his father's ability to run an efficient farm and to show profits, albeit sometimes small, in a difficult economy. Roy told me that his father planned his time carefully. If something was needed at a store in Taunton, he did not rush there to pick up just one item, as some might do, and thus neglect some farm task, but would wait until several items were needed and take care of them all in one trip. Roy recalled such a trip he made for his father to Taunton in 1911 when he was twelve years old. The main purpose of the trip was to bring a set of harnesses for repair to the harness maker in the livery stable on Court Street, but aiming to accomplish as much as possible on one trip, his father would tell Roy also to pick up a keg of nails at Washburn Hardware or go over to Pierce Hardware on Main Street for some other farm supplies. Roy remembered, too, how over and over his father would remind him and his brothers that when a job is finished not to just throw the tool being used into the shed corner, but to clean it off and hang it up where it belongs. In that way it would be ready to use when needed again. Time was important to Mr. Horton. Roy recalled that his father during the summer was up at 4 a.m., before dawn, and during the winter was in bed by 7 p.m. The farm was his whole life and he loved working around the place.

Roy was also deeply impressed with his father's determination and strength of character when he encountered a difficult or trying situation. One such time came when tragedy struck the family and the Hortons' oldest son Harlan died of tuberculosis on December 17, 1910, at age 19. Harlan had been stricken with the dread disease and to attempt a cure, had been staying the seven days before his death at a sanitarium run by Dr. Millet in East Bridgewater. Unfortunately the disease began to progress rapidly and since it soon became apparent that he had not long to live, Henry went over to the sanitarium and brought his son home. Five days later, early in the morning Harlan died. The weather had been quite cold and since the frost was deep in the ground, a grave could not be opened until spring. There being no temporary burial vault available, Henry, after the funeral service in the Horton farmhouse, took his son's

Pierce Hardware Co.,

SUCCESSORS TO

P. W. HEWINS.

NO. 8 UNION BLOCK, TAUNTON, MASS.

Builder's and General Hardware,

Paints, Oils and Varnishes.

SPORTING GOODS.

We are wholesale and retail agents for the following brands of the American Powder Mills Powder.

DEAD SHOT, DUCK AND SEA SHOOTING.

RIFLE CARTRIDGE AND TELEGRAPH POWDER.

Will sell at same price as other powder. When such concerns as Winchester Repeating Arms Co. and others of as good reputation recommend it, you can rely on its being one of the best. Send for circular. Also a large stock of Shot Shells, Wads, etc., and such other accessories that go with a gunner's outfit for sale at the very bottom price.

Spring 1888.

We are now prepared for the Spring Trade, with a complete assortment of

Builders' Hardware!
Carpenters' Tools,

Plows, Cultivators, Hoes, Rakes, Forks, Shovels,

POULTRY NETTING,

REFRIGERATORS,

Window screens, Door screens,

Salem White Lead,

Pure Linseed Oil,

Colors of all kinds, Turpentine, Varnishes, Shellac, Fishing Tackle and Gunning Goods.

☞ Largest stock in the city to select from. Please give us a call. We will sell you at low prices.

F. R. WASHBURN,

15 Union Block, Taunton.

The Pierce Hardware Store has been completely renovated to modern standards and is presently occupied by the Taunton Antique Center.

body in the coffin over to an unused vegetable storage cellar on his brother Gaius's farm on Williams Street in Dighton for storage during the winter months. When spring came, Henry and his hired man loaded the coffin on the farm wagon, proceeded to the family burial plot in the Westville section of Taunton, dug the grave, and buried the body themselves.

A grandson of Henry, Harlan Horton (1929-1991), lived on the Horton farm as a boy with his parents and grandparents. Harlan recalled that his grandfather Henry was very reserved, generally unemotional, mild mannered, and rarely spoke to his grandchildren. However, this was not the case when one day Harlan was caught by his grandfather in the barn fooling with the cows by dribbling grain in front of them. Henry had suddenly appeared from around the corner and when he saw what Harlan was doing, he exploded with anger. Harlan remembered he was careful not to repeat that transgression again.

During the early 1900's, the rural economy in the area was generally depressed, partly because small towns like Rehoboth and Dighton were still very isolated. Cars were becoming more common but their cost made them unavailable to country people until later in the 1920's. The horse and wagon (often called the "democrat wagon") or buggy were the general means of transportation. Bicycles had now become common enough and Roy was able to purchase a second hand model. Roy remarked that people had little money, that they really had nothing, and some barely got by. Until transportation improved, there was no way to obtain steady factory employment unless people moved to the city or were lucky enough to be living along a trolley line on which they could commute. Their small farms produced little; extra money was earned mostly by seasonal work on a farm or by working at a trade such as carpentry, masonry, or painting.

THE MARBLE DAIRY CO. SIGN

Chapter III

FARMING IN THE EARLY 1900's

Each morning, seven days a week, the Hortons' democrat wagon was loaded with ten quart milk cans full of the last night's and that morning's milk and delivered to the Charles C. Marble Dairy at the corner of Williams Street and Maple Street in Dighton. In 1900 Charles (1853-1943) Marble had begun a dairy farm here which had been quickly expanded into one of the most successful home delivery dairies in the Dighton - Taunton area. The Marble family not only delivered bottled milk to Taunton homes from their own dairy cows, but as their business grew, bought additional milk from the surrounding farms in Dighton, Rehoboth, and even as far away as Freetown. Some of the local farms who supplied the Marbles with milk, besides the Hortons', were the William B. Reed Farm at the site of the present Reed Farms at the corner of Williams Street and Horton Street in Dighton; the Henry E. Horton Farm on Wellington Street in Dighton opposite Horton Street; the Laneway Farm off Burt Street in Taunton, operated by the Chafee family, where the present United States Senator John Chafee of Rhode Island as a boy spent his summers; the Lester Waterman Farm at the corner of New Street and County Street in Rehoboth; the M. G. Rose Market Gardening and Dairy Farm, 116 William Street, in Dighton; the Spring Hill Farm in Assonet, part of Freetown, owned by Joseph Simmons; the Segregansett Farm operated by Wilson H. Pierce; the Briggs Farm on Briggs Street in Dighton, operated by Dr. J. Emmons Briggs who had a medical practice at 477 Beacon Street in Boston; the Albert Vandenberg Farm at the corner of Cedar Street and Simmons Street in Rehoboth; and the Samuel Smith Farm on Francis Street in Rehoboth.

According to Roy, the Marbles' Dairy had an excellent reputation for selling quality milk and the Marbles pretty much controlled milk sales in Taunton for many years. Their milk was never watered down as it sometimes was by unscrupulous dealers. They sold good milk and had a good business. During the 1920's the Marbles supplied the Weir Grammar School in Taunton with small bottles of milk under a milk program for children. Old Marble Dairy records contain letters from the school praising the milk's quality. One letter dated November 23, 1925, states in part: "We have nothing but compliments so far" [for your milk]. Another letter from the principal of the Weir School the same year notes, "Everybody is praising the quality of your products." The Marble Dairy was progressive and was one of the first, if not the first dairy to pasteurize its milk in the early 1920's. Pasteurizing had been started voluntarily by the Marbles before it was required by the pasteurization laws in Massachusetts.

In the early decades of this century the Marbles used for home deliveries some elaborately equipped milk wagons arranged with special shelves and racks for their bottles and cans. In winter time after a heavy snow storm with many roads unplowed it sometimes was difficult to make the door to door deliveries. Then, instead of wagons they would use pungs (a type of sleigh) pulled by teams of horses. It was always difficult sledding the pungs up Williams Street on the unplowed roadway, but it became easier once Winthrop Street (presently Route 44) in Taunton was reached. The Eastern Massachusetts Street Railway Company, which ran trollies from Providence to Taunton along that route through Rehoboth and Dighton, had equipped some of their cars with snow plows to keep their tracks free of the deep snow. To accommodate the local farmers, the Company let the farmers, including the Marbles, run their pungs down the plowed tracks into Taunton. The Company plowed out turnouts at regular intervals for the pungs to turn off onto in case a trolley was encountered. No matter what the weather, the Marbles had a reputation of delivering the milk to their customers everyday on time.

Roy recalled accompanying his father or brothers many times when the Hortons' milk was being delivered to the Marble Dairy. Roy explained that the Marbles were in the retail end of

Marble Dairy Wagons in the 200th Anniversary Parade of the founding of Dighton, July 1912. The pictures were taken looking up Main Street from the corner of Elm Street,

Palmer and Clifford Marble and Bertram and Frederick Wyatt and friend.

Clifford Marble, Betram and Frederick Wyatt, and other dairy employees.

the milk business, "where the money was." Roy's father sold milk delivered at their dairy for 4 1/2 cents a quart but the Marbles got over twice that for bottling it and selling it door to door. This was during the early 1900's. Later the local farmers were paid considerably more; in 1928 just before the Marble Dairy went out of business the wholesale price was 7 1/2 cents to 8 cents a quart.

Of course the Marbles, acting as the middlemen, had expensive bottling machinery to purchase and maintain at the farm as well as other specialized equipment not commonly seen on farms in the early 1920's. For example, to run the milk bottling equipment, electricity was required. At the time the Dairy was operating, none was available on Williams Street, so a makeshift arrangement had to be set up. A generator was purchased and driven by a farm tractor to supply the power to run the Dairy. Both the farm house at the Dairy and at the Palmer Marble (1896-1955) house across the street took advantage of this source of power and had a few light bulbs hooked into the system for illumination. However, recalled Evelyn Holden Elting, Palmer Marble's daughter, promptly at 9:00 each night, the generator would be shut off and the lights went out. The family then had to go back to using kerosene lamps or more likely just went to bed.

Being in the retail end of the milk business, the Marbles had the aggravation of taking the customers' complaints which the Hortons and other suppliers were spared. Once in the middle of the morning during a blizzard the Marbles received a call from an irate woman in Taunton who wanted to know why her milk had not been delivered as usual by 10:00 a.m. It was her breakfast time and she wanted her milk. The Dairy replied that the deliveries could have been delayed by the storm and that the lady should check her front step rather than the back steps where the milk was usually placed, just in case the snow was too deep in her yard for the delivery to be made at the rear door. Sure enough, upon checking her front door she found the milk had been delivered; thus was maintained the Marble tradition of delivering the milk daily as scheduled despite the weather.

The Hortons and other milk suppliers had to plan their wholesale milk deliveries to the Marbles in accordance with

The C. C. Marble Dairy Farm at the corner of Williams Street and Maple Street Dighton. Circa 1910.

Same view today.

the Marble Dairy's needs. According to Roy, not so much milk was needed by the Marbles during the summer months, either because people were away on vacation or because customers had difficulty keeping it for any length of time because of the inadequate refrigeration of that time. To complicate the situation, the dairy cows at the farm gave the most milk during the summer when grazing on the green grass, just when milk was needed the least at the Dairy. To counter this situation, Roy's father and other farmers planned farm activities so as to sell the most milk during the winter months. To do so they planned to breed their cows to calve in late summer or early fall. The milking herd was reduced in summer by letting a certain number of low producing cows dry up. For two or three months each summer the portion of the herd that was dry was placed in several pastures around West Dighton or East Rehoboth which were either owned or rented by the Hortons. The cows in these pastures were left pretty much to themselves all summer until the approach of calving time. Then an eye was kept on them to note when a calf was about to be dropped. After the birth, the new born calf was placed in the back of a wagon and driven to the farm. The mother, concerned about her calf, always followed along behind with little urging. Roy remembered one time at the Marble Dairy hearing Mr. C. C. Marble telling his father: "Henry, see if you can get a little more butter fat in the milk; my customers want to see a little more cream in their bottles." Father replied: "This is the way it is, take it or leave it. I do not want to bother with any finicky Jersey cows on my farm to get the additional butter fat." Mr. Horton preferred the predictability and steadiness of the Holstein cow. Mr. Marble never pressed the issue.

    Roy's father recalled that when he was a boy, the extra milk the cows produced in May and June was often processed into butter and stored in the cellar for later use or sold. That use of the surplus milk was no longer practical when Roy was a boy, because low priced butter and cheese had become available from efficient commercial creameries in such states as Maine, Wisconsin, New York, and Vermont; cheap rail transportation now allowed these products to be shipped inexpensively into Massachusetts.

    Roy recalled that the economics of dairying on the Horton

farm went like this: during the winter most of their 24 cows were milking and producing 24 cans of milk at 10 quarts per can per day or 240 quarts a day. But during the summer only 11 cows were milked, giving 110 quarts per day. The income during the winter was about $11.00 per day or $77.00 per week, but in the summer the gross income was about one half that. Roy recalled that this really was not much, considering all the grain needed to feed the cows, the farm equipment that had to be purchased and repaired, extra labor required to help with haying and harvesting the corn, and money needed just for living expenses. (Additional dairy economics, Appendix III.)

As trucks began coming into use during the 1920's, local dairymen found it more convenient to hire someone with a motorized vehicle to pick up their milk each morning and deliver it to the Marble Dairy. For several years during the late 1920's, D. Lee Johnson of Anawan Street, Rehoboth, was contracted to make those deliveries. Early each morning he made pickups beginning at the Benjamin Munroe farm, Chestnut Street, Dighton, and continuing along to the Jason Waterman farm at Wheeler's Corner, Rehoboth; the Elwood Horton farm, New Street, Rehoboth; the Lester Waterman farm, Perry's Corner, Rehoboth; the Ernest L. Horton farm, Wellington Street, Dighton; the Henry and Raymond Horton farm, Wellington Street, Dighton; the Dighton Poor farm owned by Mr. Rodrigues, Smith Street, Dighton; the Gaius Horton farm, Williams Street, Dighton; the Araujo Brothers farm, Williams Street, Dighton; and the Joshua Reed farm, Williams Street. The Waterman, Araujo, and Reed farms were small operations with only a few cows, producing only about 50 or 60 quarts of milk per day. Today not one of those places has a dairy cow on it and only at the Ernest L. Horton farm, Henry and Raymond Horton farm, and the Elwood Horton farm are the old dairy barns still standing. The Araujo farm and the Reed farm, however, were many years ago converted into truck garden farms that operate very successfully to this day.

Like many other businesses, when the Great Depression began in 1929, the Marble Dairy encountered economic difficulties. Many customers had to drop home milk deliveries or had trouble paying their milk bills to the dairy. About 1932 the Marbles were forced to close their doors and the Hortons began delivering their milk to the Lincoln Dairy on North Walker Street, Taunton, Massachusetts.

The farming season for the Hortons began in the fields after the mud had dried up enough in the spring to allow the spreading of the manure that had accumulated through the winter in the barn cellar. Roy recalled how during the winter manure was dropped into the barn cellar through scuttles in the manure gutter in the barn floor. By spring time the barn cellar would be full and the manure was ready to be loaded by hand on to tip carts for spreading on the fields. Around 1890, Roy's father bought a horse drawn manure spreader from a company in Worcester, Massachusetts, one of the first manure spreaders to be used in this area. Unfortunately it had been designed poorly with high wooden wheels that made the body too high to get it under the barn. It was easy to spread the manure with it, once it was loaded, but the problem was loading it. Since the spreader would not fit under the barn, the manure had to be first thrown out from the cellar, then shoveled again into the spreader, all by hand. Roy's father soon gave up using it because it was just too much work and returned to the old way of using the farm tip cart. John, the hired man, would yoke the oxen to the big tip cart and back it under the barn where he and Mr. Horton would load it up by hand, using manure forks. John would then drive the oxen out on to Wellington Street, perhaps turning left toward the fields on Smith Street. Once the rig was heading in the right direction, he would climb up on the pole or tongue of the wagon and ride while the oxen would plod along by themselves. When he reached the field to be manured, he would jump off and direct the oxen in through the gate. After dumping the load, which was easily done by releasing a simple tripping device that allowed the body to tip back by its own weight, he would repeat the ride back to the barn. Meanwhile Henry would be working around the farm on other tasks; when John returned, Henry would drop whatever he was doing and help John put on another load. After the piles had been dumped evenly across the field, the next step was to scatter the piles over the land with a manure fork. Roy recalled that sometimes the manure was laid on so thick that consequently the timothy hay would grow as high as your head and the horse-drawn mower would have trouble getting started to cut it.

After the fields that were to be planted for that year were plowed, harrowed, and seeded and the crops were well started, the cultivation of corn was begun. Much of the farm work during June was spent on weeding and hoeing field corn. First the corn was weeded by a single horse drawing the cultivator down the corn rows, guided by Roy or one of his brothers. When the task was completed, Henry with his sons and John the hired man would each take a row of corn and proceed through the field hoeing around the plants and chopping out the weeds that the cultivator missed. This procedure was carried out about three times during the month with the last cultivation being completed near the 4th of July.

Roy told me that when he was a boy, haying usually began the day after the 4th of July and that it took the better part of that month to complete. Today haying is begun as early in June as possible, often before the 15th. Because there is a lot of moisture in the young grass in June — and it is usually a wet month — the farmers of Roy's boyhood, who had only horse drawn mowing machines and hay rakes, had difficulty drying the hay properly at that early date. With modern hay equipment, the early date is possible, mainly because of the hay conditioner that squeezes the juice out of the hay stems as it is being cut. Early cut hay is succulent and of much higher quality than the mature dried out grasses cut in July.

When Roy was a boy, it was possible to buy at the farm supply store many varieties of hay seed which would grow into good quality hay. Roy's grandfather had said that, according to the Pauls, back in the 1700's and into the early 1800's there was little good hay seed available. The importing of timothy seed from England in the early nineteenth century marked the beginning of good hay crops. Also, chemical fertilizer to supplement the manure was not generally available until the latter part of the nineteenth century. This lack of good seed and fertilizer is why the hay crop was limited to only half or three quarters of a ton per acre during those early times whereas two tons per acre is common today. Hay was still in short supply when Roy was a boy and every little field, patch, and door yard was either a pasture or mowed. Roy noted that hay did grow naturally here, but even if it was fertilized it was still of very poor quality when compared to imported varieties.

When every blade of grass was important. A typical scene of cows grazing in the front yard.

The bottom picture was taken in 1896 of a house in the Homestead Avenue area of Rehoboth and the location of the other picture is unknown.

When Roy's father was a boy, all hay was cut with a scythe. At that time, usually on the bigger farms, cutting was done by a gang of men with the best mower setting the pace, leading the other mowers around and around the field. However, during Roy's boyhood horse drawn mowing machines were common on the larger farms and the Hortons had one too. Even though the mowing machines had supplanted the hard work of mowing with a scythe, there was still one tedious task to be performed in mowing which was usually assigned to one of the younger boys on the farm. At the end of the sickle bar of the mower there was a grass board attached horizontally and at a right angle to the bar to tip the cut grass in toward the mower. This board left a clear strip with no grass about ten or twelve inches wide to prevent the heel or the inside end of the cutter bar from clogging up with the newly cut grass on its next trip around the field. Since this arrangement did not always work properly and clogging did occur, Roy or one of his brothers was selected to follow the mowing machine around and around the field with a pitch fork to throw aside hay lying in the cleared strip. When occasionally the cutter bar jammed up with hay, the boy following had to do the unclogging. Following the mower was usually a morning long task and never looked forward to by Roy or his brothers.

Harlan Horton (1929-1991), a boy of the next generation growing up on the farm, also had that job. He recalled that a strange diversion occasionally occurred to interrupt the monotony of following the mower. Sometimes a pheasant hiding in the grass was not quick enough to fly up as the mower approached and had his legs severed by the sickle bar. As the bird would fly away with the stubs of its legs dripping blood, Harlan remembered feeling sorry for it and wondered what ever happened to the bird afterward. He also recalled there was danger of his own finger being badly cut or severed on the sharp knives of the sickle bar when he tried to untangle the clogged knives. The boys were cautioned not to do this job with the hand but by poking out the tangled grass with a stick.

The Hortons also had a horse drawn hay rake that gathered up the cured cut hay in large tines. The operator riding on the rake at the desired moment would trip the rake and cause the hay to be dumped into a windrow. Some farms also had a horse drawn hay tedder that had reciprocating forks moving in such a way as to imitate a pitch fork turning over the hay. Hay tedding was done after the hay had become wet from a shower or if it was so thick that it was drying poorly. Roy's father did not have this machine; so he did his tedding by hand with pitch forks. When a field needed tedding, after dinner everyone on the farm including the men, boys, and sometimes women would take a pitch fork, line up in a row on the outside of the field, and begin to work their way around the lot fluffing up and turning over the hay. If there were a number of workers, the task would soon be completed; in fact, it seemed to Roy that everyone met in the middle of the field in no time. Even though mowing and raking had become mechanized on the Horton farm, scythes and wooden hand rakes were still used. After the mowing machine had completed its work, Mr. Horton, hired man John, and the older sons took out their scythes and mowed all around the rocks, along the walls and fences, and into any corners that the horse mower missed. After the hay dried and had been raked by the horse rake into windrows, hand rakes were used to rake those same hard-to-get places to be sure nothing was wasted.

Besides the horse drawn hay rake and mower, the only other mechanical aid used by the Hortons was a horse operated hay fork. The fork was an implement that made the unloading of the hay wagon at the barn a much easier task. One end of a rope was fastened to a horse stationed in the farm yard while the other end was passed through a pulley high up under the barn roof and tied on to the hay fork. After the heavy iron fork was closed up and dropped into the pile of hay on the wagon, the horse was urged forward. The pull on the rope opened the fork and lifted up a good sized hay load off the wagon. The horse pulled the hay high up over the mow where a man was waiting to trigger the release mechanism, to drop the hay where it was wanted. This fork did away with the tedious job of pitching off the hay with pitch forks from the wagon and throwing it overhead into the mow.

As the trend continued for the local farms to be more and more mechanized, Roy noted that his father resisted making this type of improvement and generally preferred doing things the old way by hand. Perhaps he learned this conservatism from his father James H. Horton who also had a reputation for keeping the old methods. When James still owned the Paul farm, a local newspaper in July, 1888, commented on the subject: "J. H. Horton has a barn full of hay and all nicely secured. He for the first time has consented to save a little hand labor by the purchase of a horse fork, which works to a good advantage and puts the hay into the mow with the power of the horse."

To ensure having enough hay to last all winter, after the barn was full, extra hay was cut and stored in two big hay stacks in the farm yard on the south side of the barn. Mr. Horton never bought hay or sold any of his manure. Buying hay showed poor planning and farm management, recalled Roy, and selling manure would just be robbing yourself of fertilizer needed for next year's crop. Occasionally if there was a surplus of hay, it was sold, but Roy's father did not consider that good farm practice because the manure that it would have produced from feeding it to the cows would be lost to the farm.

Roy noted that certain lots were known for growing the best crops of hay. The Grintry Lot on the Paul Lane was always a good hay lot. The Jesse Goff lot also on the lane would produce five loads of hay (2 1/2 tons). The Square Lot and the Grintry were often used for growing strawberries. Answering my question about the origin of the Grintry Lot's name, Roy thought that it was probably once called the Green Tree Lot and over the years had became contracted to Grintry.

When tractors began to replace the horse during the 1940's, the rockier fields had to be abandoned for farming or have the stones pushed out with a bulldozer. According to Roy, many of the fields that his father cultivated with a horse were too rocky for a modern tractor with its farm equipment to operate efficiently and safely. With a well trained horse, a farmer could slide his plow or cultivator right around a stone. If the implements did hook up on a rock, the horse would stop as soon as it felt the strain, whereas with the clumsy but powerful tractor this was impossible. When a plow being pulled by a tractor struck a stone, the tractor would try to keep on going and often break something before it could be stopped. The tractor had "no give." The first lots to be cleared of rocks by a bulldozer on the Horton farm were the Grintry and Peach Tree Lots. In 1946 when Raymond was operating the farm he hired a bulldozer to push the stones from these lots over to the edge of the field, and by burying the old wall between the lots he joined them into one. Raymond was one of the first farmers in Dighton to hire a bulldozer for land clearing as soon as they became available for this type of work after World War II.

Some lots were so rough with rocks or the soil was so thin that bulldozing was not practical and they could only be used for pasture. One such lot was the Tinkham farm. When Roy was a boy the Tinkham family owned this farm located behind the Hortons' farm on Smith Street. They had a son, Percy, who was a life time friend of Roy, almost like a brother. Eventually, in 1928, Henry Horton bought this farm from the Tinkhams, but it was so stony it was used only for grazing land. Roy said that there were so many stones on it you couldn't put a fence post in the ground. The Tinkhams had had it under cultivation for a number of years, mainly raising plants to sell. As the plants were sold, some of the loam went with the roots, thus gradually decreasing the depth of the top soil. Even though the farm gradually lost its top soil, the Tinkhams were considered to be progressive farmers. They not only did a large business with the sale of plants, but they also operated a cannery to process their own and neighbors' vegetables. A steam boiler was set up on their farm for this purpose.

After purchasing the farm, the Hortons never occupied the old Tinkham house, and only used it occasionally to house some of their migrant farm workers and wood cutters. The barn was used to shelter the Horton dry cows and heifers and to store a little hay for summer feeding when the pastures became dried out in late August. Both the barn and the house eventually burned to the ground. The house was first to go while being occupied by two wood cutters employed by the Hortons, Ted and Jean Arsenault. Vandals, it was thought, eventually torched the barn. Roy's nephew, Harlan Horton, recalled once trying to "bog harrow" a piece of the Tinkham farm to prepare the soil for planting some new pasture grass. He found so little loam there that the harrow could only scratch the soil. When Roy saw the ground being churned up in 1987 during the construction project to build the Fieldstone Drive plat, he remarked that in his opinion the soil on that farm had not changed one bit. He also noted while visiting there that since his nephew

Harlan Horton had removed a lot of gravel from the site, the looks of the farm had not improved and that he now hardly recognized the place.

Because of the shortage of hay, fresh meadow hay was very important to the farmer, particularly in the eighteenth and much of the nineteenth century. Fresh meadow hay grew both in swamps that had been cleared of trees and in swamps that were naturally free of trees and brush. In the early days the treeless swamps were much in demand because no clearing of trees and brush had to be done to get a crop of hay. Salt meadow hay for the same reason was also in demand, but the Hortons had none. Roy said that about one half of the Horton hay crop came from the fresh meadows. Because it was not a high quality hay, his father would use some for the dry cows, enough for one feed a day. His father told Roy that when he was little, cows were lucky to get even fresh meadow hay to eat because that was about all the hay some farmers had. Roy added that now cows are picky, just like people, because they are used to better things to eat. Not only cows but people in those days ate poorly too: salt pork, corn, potatoes, and rye were the farmers' winter food.

The last of August and first weeks of September were the time for fresh meadow haying because it was cooler then and the swamps were still generally dry before the fall rains began. However, hornets and yellow jackets who liked to nest in the ground in the swamps were fearsome in some years. Roy remembered his father getting stung all over when his scythe cut too near one of the nests. Occasionally large snakes were encountered, but they were no bother, at least when compared to the hornets. Since the ground was too rough and swampy for the horse drawn machine to be used, all cutting had to be done with the scythe, a very hot, tedious job.

Roy remembered when he was nine or ten years old (about 1911) going with his father and the hired men to cut hay in the fresh meadows along the Segregansett River off Burt Street in Taunton at what is now known as the Laneway Farm. His father and four or five of the hired men early in the morning loaded up the democrat wagon with their scythes and rakes and with Roy rode together over to the Laneway Farm with an extra horse tied behind the wagon. Mr. Horton and his men worked there all day cutting down the rough swamp grass with their scythes. Roy stayed a while, trying to do what work he was able to do at that age, but after a few hours he would return home riding horseback on the extra horse.

Another place the Hortons cut fresh meadow hay was at a lot called the "Old Slough" on the south side of Horton Street where the high voltage wires and gas line now cross the street. It was a huge fresh meadow with a pond hole on the west side. Cows grazing on grandfather James Horton's farm used to come to that pond to drink. Roy himself cleaned out the pond once. Later when the New England Power came through in 1960 with its transmission lines, dirt and debris were pushed into the pond. Roy insisted that the Company clean it up and it did.

Roy remembered in 1911, when he was twelve years old, that he and his brother Elwood mowed and raked that whole fresh meadow by hand. The cutting was done by scythes and raking done with wooden hand rakes. After the grass had dried it was raked up into cocks. Roy then helped his brother pole the haystacks out. To do that two light cedar poles were shoved under a cock from opposite directions and the pile lifted up in stretcher fashion with Roy on one end and Elwood on the other. The two would then walk or stumble with the load over the swamp tufts of grass to the landing place near the water hole. When enough hay had been gathered, they loaded it onto a wagon, hauled it home, and pitched it onto a large hay stack at the stack yard just south of the barn. This hay being of poor quality, much of it ended up as bedding or strawberry bed mulch. Sometimes a certain variety of this grass did make fairly good feed. Roy remembered that it was an awful job, cutting and lugging all that hay by hand: "People today don't know what hard work is"

Roy described the family orchard for me. Every farm, he said, had at least a few apple trees. Apples were grown for eating and for cider. The Hortons' orchard was on Smith Street where Raymond Rose now lives. This lot, called the Vineyard, was very rocky and not suitable for cultivation. It was next to a small pond known as Devil's Pond. Just west of it was Four Acre Lot that could be cultivated because it was fairly free of stone; cabbage was often grown here. These lots, the Vineyard, the Four Acre lot, Devil's Pond, and also the Grintry and Peach Tree Orchard, were all part of the original Paul farm; some of them had also been used for orchards by earlier generations. When Roy was old enough, he was given the job of tending the fruit trees on the orchard lot. Several times during the growing season he used to spray the trees with a mixture of arsenate of lead, copper sulphate, and something called black leaf. These chemicals were very toxic and would not be allowed now, but at age 85 Roy noted that somehow he had survived them all.

Roy recalled that the best tasting eating apple was the Seek-No-Further. The Hortons had just one tree of that variety from which Roy's mother made some delicious applesauce. Some of the poorer apples and drops were taken to the cider press where they were pressed into cider. The cider was stored in barrels for the winter in the cellar under the wagon shed attached to the barn near the house. When the Hortons and the hired men came back in the late afternoon from working in the woods in the winter, a drink of cider was always looked forward to, either hard or sweet.

Another orchard Roy often mentioned was the Bosworth Orchard, an outlying lot located on the northerly side of the Tinkham Farm. Since the land was covered with large oak trees, it had no resemblance to an orchard. When I asked Roy why what was obviously a woodlot was called an orchard, he replied that his father said that someone named Bosworth once had an orchard here, probably back in Grandfather Paul's day. Roy never saw any signs of an orchard there, but he noted that once a lot got a name it seemed to stick forever, even though the original use had entirely changed. The Peach Tree Lot at the lane was still known by that name, but there had not been a peach picked from there in years. The same went for the Case Orchard further down the lane where Roy never saw an apple.

When he was young, Roy continued, corn was grown for two purposes. Some was grown to be chopped up, ear, stalk, and all, and then blown into the silo for silage; other corn was left standing in the field until the ears had dried sufficiently to be husked and stored in the corn crib. The silage process was rather a recent innovation on the Horton farm. Silage was juicy and succulent and the cows loved it, but the dried ears of corn after being ground were not so digestible or desirable. The corn to be used for silage was cut in late August or early September when it was mature but still green. There were no corn chopping machines pulled by tractors like those used today. The harvesting was done by men walking between two rows of corn, cutting the stalks off on both rows with a corn knife and dropping the stalks behind. Another method sometimes used to cut off the corn stalks was to have a worker strap a sharp blade to his shoe and cut off the stalk by kicking it with the blade. The advantage of this method was that both hands were free to grasp and pile the stalks. After the corn was cut and laid into piles, the stalks were pitched onto a wagon and hauled to the silo at the barn for unloading. Here the Hortons kept the only gasoline powered piece of machinery they owned, a corn blower. As the stalks were fed into a hopper they were chopped, ear and all, into small pieces by the machine and blown up a pipe into the silo through an opening in the roof. In Roy's younger days this machine was run by a one cylinder gasoline engine, but later the power take off on a Fordson tractor was used. Roy remembered the tractor engine's big radiator blowing off clouds of steam on a hot day as it strained to drive the machine.

A machine called a corn binder later became available to make the task of cutting and piling the corn easier. Henry Horton, although always reluctant to invest in labor saving machinery, eventually bought one. The binder was drawn by a team of horses or a tractor if one was available. As it went down the corn rows, the machine cut off the stalks close to the ground and gathered them on to the binder into a bundle. When the operator decided the bundle was large enough, he threw a lever which caused the machine to tie the bundle with twine and eject it to the ground. The bundles were later picked up in the wagon, or in later years in a truck, for hauling to the silo. Ernest L. Horton of Wellington Street, Dighton, recalled that as a young man he sometimes was employed at the Horton farm to help with the corn harvest. He said that it was very hard work for the hired men to lift the corn bundles with pitch forks and to throw them into the wagon. Also, if the bundles were not placed just right on the silage blower, the corn would jam the blower and make considerable additional work to clear the machine. When tractor power corn choppers that did the chopping right in the field became available, the Hortons were quick to purchase one and get rid of the binder. With no regrets, they sold it to Abbott Thayer, father of the well known Taunton surgeon, the late Dr. Thayer, for use at his Pavilion Farm on Tremont Street, Taunton.

The corn to be stored as ears in the corn crib was handled in Roy's boyhood just as it had been for generations of the Horton and Paul families. Roy described to me the corn harvesting in detail. When the ears and stalks had dried sometime in October, his father, John, Roy, his brothers, and anyone else they could find to help would begin cutting the corn stalks by grasping the tops of several stalks at once with the left hand and reaching down with the corn knife in the right hand to cut the stalks off close to the ground. The stalks were then placed up against previously cut stalks. When enough had been gathered the tops were tied together in what was called a stook. The stooked corn was allowed to dry further until sometime during November when a bench was set up out in the field on the lee side of the stook and the husking was begun. The husked corn was put in the corn crib and stalks were rebundled and stored under cover in the barn. The stalks were known as corn stover. To rip open the husks the men used a husking peg, a small hook sewn on to a leather pad that was tied to the palm of the hand. Roy recalled that it was always a cold job sitting out in the field husking in November.

During the winter, young Roy was sometimes assigned the task of loading the democrat wagon with the ear corn from the crib and carting it to the water powered grist mill in the Perryville section of Rehoboth for grinding. The mill had a machine that smashed up the ears of corn, cob and kernels together, and ground them into feed to be used for the cows' winter grain. Mr. Horton often used to buy a bag of whole corn from the feed store and have the miller grind it in with the corn cob meal to make a richer mixture. Although the grain was nothing like the carefully prepared grain mixtures available today, Roy said that the cows did eat it and liked it. However, the corn stover that had been saved after the husking had been completed was another matter. The stover was dried out, tough for the cows to chew and of little food value. The cows disliked this feed even more than fresh meadow hay. A lot

The Grist Mill at Perryville in Rehoboth circa 1910. Here the Hortons brought their corn to be ground into cattle feed.

Tha same view today. The race to the mill still runs in front of the present Robert Armstrong House, seen at the rear of the picture.

E. Otis Dyer stands at the Mill Dam at Perryville. The stone dam is at the left and the race to the Mill is on the right.

of the stalks, like the fresh meadow hay, ended up as bedding for the cows, after the cows had finished throwing them around and picking them over.

Roy's father told Roy that in his boyhood it was the custom on the Horton farm and other local farms to feed the cows after they came in the barn in the fall first the dried corn stalks, considered to be the poorest feed; oat straw, considered to be a little more palatable, was fed next; fresh meadow hay, rated the third best fodder, was then given; English or upland hay, by far the best quality fodder, was saved for last during the late winter season. The theory was that since the cattle were fat after being out in the pastures all summer, they could stand eating the poor feed in the fall better than later in the winter; by late winter they had thinned down considerably and by then were in need of more nourishing food to get through the season. This procedure was necessary because there just was not enough of the quality English hay available to carry the cattle through to spring, so every type of forage had to be utilized.

Corn was also run through a hand cranked sheller to separate the kernels from the cob and then fed to the chickens and turkeys. This job was usually delegated to one of the younger boys on the farm. Harlan Horton remembered that when he was growing up on the farm during the 1930's, one of his Saturday jobs was to shell enough corn to fill a fifty gallon drum—enough to feed his fathers's flock of turkeys through the following week.

Carrying on a tradition begun by grandfather James H. Horton in the decades after the Civil War, succeeding generations of Hortons, like most other successful local farmers, depended on raising and selling vegetables for a portion of their cash income. Cabbage was always a popular crop, often grown to pay the real estate taxes on the farm in the fall. Each year after a large amount of cow manure was spread on the lot, the cabbage sometimes would grow so fast that the cabbage moth could not eat it fast enough to do any real damage. Roy remembered how his father trusted him from about age twelve to drive a wagon full of cabbages into the wholesale market in Providence: he would start from home about one o'clock in the morning and arrive at the wholesaler about five o'clock. On the way home he would stop in East Providence to feed the horse and arrive back at the farm about ten thirty in the morning: "then after putting the horse away, I'd eat then, and go out to play. That was quite a responsibility for a youngster." It is hard today to imagine when the heavy truck and auto traffic is now observed on Winthrop Street (Route 44) that there were once many horse drawn wagons plodding along that road to and from the market in Providence, many of them driven by young farm boys.

Strawberries were another cash crop that the Hortons grew each year. The Square Lot on the old Paul farm lane was often used for this purpose. A small building had been erected on this lot to house strawberry equipment and offer a place for the strawberry workers to get out of the rain from a sudden thunder shower. Strawberries were grown in large quantities by Dighton farmers when Roy was a boy. Much of the crop grown in the central and eastern part of Dighton was carted to the train station in south Dighton, loaded upon the nightly special train, and sold in the Boston market. The Horton crop more often went to the Providence area.

The favorite crop of the Hortons and the one from which they made the most profit was tomatoes. Since tomatoes did not ripen all at once, they could be picked over and over again during the season. The Hortons especially attempted to hit the late tomato market by setting out the plants later than usual in the spring, hoping they would be still mostly green when the first frost came in September. The green tomatoes were picked and stored under shelter in time to be safe from the frost where they continued gradually to ripen over another four or five weeks. Farmers having tomatoes which had mostly ripened at the time of the first frost were not able to preserve many for a later market and were soon out of the tomato business for that year. When that happened the price of tomatoes would often soar; it was then that the Hortons hoped to make a "killing" in the tomato market. Once in a while this did happen; from his late tomato profits one year in the 1920's Mr. Horton was able to purchase his first car, a Model T Ford. The tomatoes had been grown on the Hathaway Lot and were sold for $3.50 per half bushel, a huge sum for those times. In 1949 another killing was made by Roy's brother, Raymond, when he made enough profit on late tomatoes to buy his first modern rubber tired International tractor. The new tractor replaced an earlier model that had been purchased by Mr. Horton in the 1920's. The latter was a heavy Fordson tractor with iron wheels, a rather impractical machine with limited use. It was sometimes used in the vegetable business to harrow the cabbage and tomato fields before planting, but because of its clumsiness, it was more often delegated to being a stationary engine, running a corn chopper and blower at the silo. Until he was no longer able, Roy continued to try to make his killing in the late tomato market. One of his last tries was with his son-in-law Fancis McClellan about 1975.

Roy enjoyed reminiscing about some of his farm chores and work. Every morning and evening he would help his father, brothers, and the hired man John milk the cows in the barn. During the summer months when the milking was completed, the cows were driven to pasture. When the pastures at the Poor Farm on the east side of Smith Street were to be grazed, there was quite a distance to walk to drive the cows to the pastures in the morning and back to the barn in the evening. When he had that task to perform, Roy worked out a system to avoid some of that walking. First he would drive the cows from the barn out on to Wellington Street and turn them left toward Smith Street. Roy then ran ahead, opened the gate at the old Paul farm lane, and headed the cows down that path toward Smith Street. Once they were well on their way the cows could usually be counted on to plod on by themselves down the lane by the Square Lot, the Rocky Lot, the Hathaway Lot, and the Four Acre Lot to the bars near the Orchard Lot at the end of the lane on Smith Street. While the cows were ambling along, Roy would return to the barn, mount his bicycle, and ride down Wellington Street, turn left on Smith Street and ride to the barway at the end of the lane on Smith Street, usually arriving just in time to let the cows out on to the street and to turn them up toward the Poor Farm lane. There was usually very little trouble keeping the herd moving in the right direction, even when by themselves, because they always seemed to know where they were going and where the best and most plentiful pastures were located, or at least the lead cow knew. Smith Street was then a narrow dirt road with a few houses on it, so there were no traffic problems. Once the cows had been let into the pasture, Roy returned to his bicycle by the Orchard Lot and pedaled home, thus saving himself the walk back. The opposite procedure was used in bringing the cows home for the evening milking. Roy later thought he was pretty clever to save all that walking.

During warmer months Roy's father used to hire extra men at 15 cents an hour to help with the planting, haying, and harvesting. The men would work a six day week from 7 a.m. to 6 p.m. with an hour off at noon, $9.00 for a full week's work. Roy used to like to go out and sit and talk with the hired help at noon time while they were eating their lunch under a large elm tree in the front yard.

Reminiscing about other work, Roy said that his father was a road commissioner for this part of Dighton around 1915 and was paid 17 1/2 cents an hour for use of his tip cart and driver. In those days road work consisted mainly of shoveling by hand the gravel from a local gravel bank on to the Horton tip cart and spreading the gravel along the washed out and deeply rutted portions of the road. Roy recalled that it was in 1913 when

ROY HORTON, FARM BOY

The hedgerow shadows had crossed the field,
In the distance was heard a moo,
There was a bicycle parked at the barway,
As the cows came clattering through.
They fanned out onto the stubbled field,
And stopped for a little bite.
But the lead cow kept on toward the barn,
In the grey of the dimming light.
Meanwhile, pedaling down the road,
Was the farmboy on his machine.
But the lead cow kept her steady trudge,
According to her routine.
Centering along a dusty rut,
The farmboy rang his bell.
As though in answer the cow bells rang,
To say that all was well.
The barn in sight, they began to trot,
The farmboy coasts to the gate.
He's timed his journey along the road,
To be sure he's never late.
The barway up, the lead cow through,
The others in a crowd.
This little system repeated each night,
Is something of which he is proud.
Decades later he would recall those times,
Inspiring books and little rhymes.
      by Betsey Dexter Dyer

he was fourteen years old that he was hired to drive a tip cart back and forth to the gravel bank when Center Street in Dighton was being re-graveled. He did this work under Samuel Davis, who lived in what is now the Dighton Historical Society building at the corner of Center Street and Williams Street.

 The old farms Roy knew of in his boyhood had many buildings big and small scattered about the farmyard, all used for some special farm purpose. Today, farmers find one or two large buildings serving several purposes to be more practical and more efficient. Often the modern farm building is constructed of metal for low maintenance costs, rather than of wood and shingles as commonly used in older outbuildings. Also, as the general type of farm became more and more mechanized and specialized as a dairy farm, such enterprises as raising poultry, growing vegetables, and shoeing oxen, were given up and the buildings associated with them gradually abandoned. Once when Roy was standing with me in my farmyard on Fairview Avenue, Rehoboth, he commented on the many farm buildings I had: "When I was a boy, that is the way all the old farms were. My father's farm once looked that way, too."

The Horton farm house was probably built by James W. Paul in the early 1800's as a 1 1/2 story Cape style cottage, 20 feet by 36 feet long. Over the years this structure was added to by the Pauls and Hortons at least four times and perhaps as many as seven times according to some people. The first major change took place during the mid 1800's when the roof of the original cottage was raised to make a 2 1/2 story house. It was then that the old center chimney with its associated fireplaces was removed. In the late nineteenth century, the ell to the south was added and the northern ell was built by Roy in 1924 to accommodate his mother and father. They had been living at another Horton farm on Winfield Lane and wished to return to the main farm. While they occupied the new quarters, their son Raymond and his family lived in the south section of the house. Raising roofs and building additions were common practices in the Dighton and Rehoboth area during the late nineteenth and early twentieth century. As the prosperity of the farmer improved along with the increased market opportunities offered in the surrounding cities and as the size of his family grew, renovations to the old house were made accordingly.

The original portion of the Horton barn was built about 1850 by the Pauls. It is a pegged beam structure now about 24 feet wide and 86 feet long, built in the New England barn style. That is, it has a main door in the gable end of the street side of the barn for the passage of wagons and a small door at the rear for the dairy herd to use when going to and from the pasture or cow yard. As dairy herds were being enlarged during the middle and later part of the nineteenth century in response to the in-

Exterior and interior views of the Horton Barn, shortly before it was rebuilt into a horse stable.

Interior of the Horton Barn before remodeling in 1992

creased marketing opportunities, this style of barn was developed to overcome the difficulties entailed by any attempt to add on to the then commonly used English style barn. Since the English barn had its main door in the center of its long side, the distance that an addition could be extended to the rear was limited to how far the slope of the existing roof could be extended rearward and still maintain sufficient head room in the barn. An expansion in a lateral direction was not practical because each new bay would require its own main door for access. In contrast a New England style barn could be fairly easily enlarged by extending the gable end of the roof and rear wall back almost an unlimited distance. Each new bay could still be serviced through the one big door by wagons running along an extension of the existing alleyway. During recent reconstruction of the Horton barn by the present owner, Thomas Horton, the framing showed that the barn had been added on to in this way.

It was also common to add a cowshed type structure to the long side of the New England style barn to gain more width on the barn floor. Near the turn of the century a twenty foot wide addition was added the full length of the south side of the

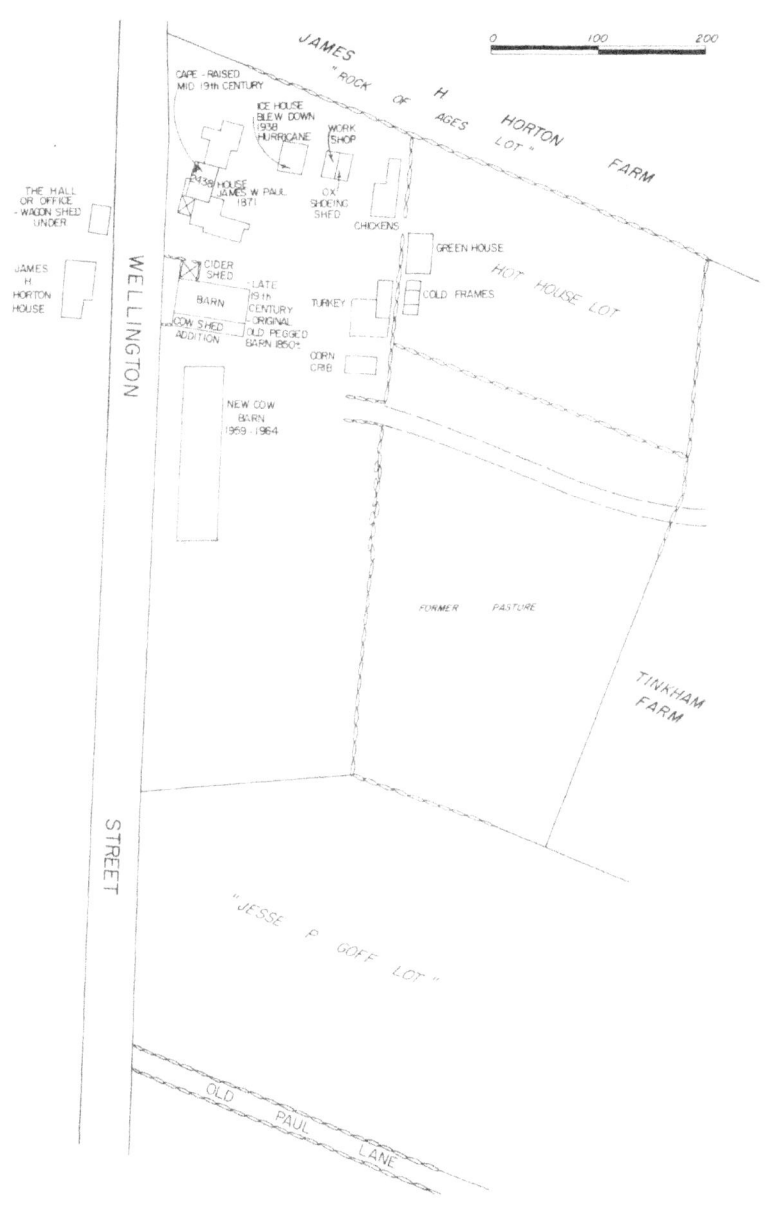

FARM BUILDINGS AT PAUL - HORTON FARM
Dighton, circa 1900

Horton barn. In 1992 this lean-to was removed.

Behind the Horton house and running parallel to the wall of the Rock of Ages Lot on the James H. Horton farm were three buildings in a row. The first was an ice house where ice that was cut by the Hortons on their small pond near the Paul lane was stored and used for cooling the milk during the summer. This building, not having been used as an ice house since 1922 when ice cutting by the Hortons was discontinued, blew down in the 1938 hurricane and was never rebuilt. Ice delivered to the farm had become available and that, along with soon to be installed electrical refrigeration, made the storage of ice no longer a necessity. Next to the ice house stood a shed that served a dual purpose: the westerly half served as a work shop and a tool storage area while the easterly portion contained a special winch and associated equipment that the Hortons used to lift an ox off the ground for shoeing. The third building was a hen house and hen yard, common on almost all the farms in the area during Roy's boyhood; feeding the poultry and picking up and handling the eggs were usually chores taken by the women of the family. To the south of the hen house was a turkey house and beyond that two more hen houses and a corn crib, sometimes known as the corn barn.

The crib was built on stone posts a couple of feet off the ground to discourage rodents from damaging the corn. After the ears of field corn were husked by hand in the late fall, they were stored here for animal feed during the winter months. Some of the corn was shelled to feed the poultry and the rest was ground, cob and all, into dairy feed at the Perryville Rehoboth grist mill for the cows. Because of the popularity of using corn for ensilage during the early 1900's and because of the trend to eliminate poultry raising and to specialize strictly in dairying, corn cribs were gradually abandoned and soon rotted away or were torn down. Today there are few cribs standing in the Dighton and Rehoboth area. Behind the turkey house, over the wall in the Hot House Lot stood the cold frames and hot house where the Hortons raised their vegetable seedlings in the early spring. Just as the corn crib was abandoned when the Hortons went into dairy specialization, so the hot house, cold frames, and poultry buildings also were neglected so that nothing of them remains today on the farm.

Another factor that hastened the removal of many small outbuildings from the Dighton and Rehoboth farms mainly during the 1950's and 1960's was the high real estate value which the local assessors placed on these buildings in relationship to land value. During that time, because land values were low, the increased taxes required to build badly needed new schools and other town improvements fell on the owners of buildings. Today when land values are high the opposite is true; land owners now pay a higher share of the tax burden. During that period of high building assessments, many people including the Hortons began tearing down non-essential buildings. I recall one day in the early 1960's standing with Roy at his grandfather James H. Horton's farmyard and listening to him complain about the new valuation on an old wood shed on the property. He had just received the assessment from a new town-wide property revaluation conducted by the Dighton tax assessors. He said he had told those assessors that they had to be crazy to put such a value on an old wood shed like that and that he would tear it down before he paid it. A few days later while I was driving by the farm I noticed that true to his word the old building was gone. This was also the period when the once numerous large poultry enterprises became very uneconomical to run and most of the huge chicken houses that had once dotted the Rehoboth and Dighton landscape were razed by their owners.

One unusual farm outbuilding which still stands on the Horton farm is the structure on the edge of Wellington Street opposite the Horton farmhouse. This building is a small sagging two story building with the first floor open and facing the street. This lower section was used for the storage of wagons and tip carts and in later years for a tractor. The upstairs of the building had been used in earlier years as a place for young people to hold dances and was called the Hall. Roy said that this section had also been called the Office, suggestive that once it may have been used for some type of farm office. In later years it was converted into a three room apartment which is now vacant.

The former James H. Horton house, circa 1870, and the Hall or Office on Wellington Street, West Dighton. Wagons were stored underneath and dances were sometimes held upstairs.

The Hall or Office

There was a shack on the west side of Paul Lane near the Rocky Lot that was generally used to store a plow overnight or give shelter to the strawberry pickers during a thunderstorm. An on going job that had to be done on the farm about every other year was to cut down the bushes and briers in the pastures that the cows did not eat. If this cutting was not done on a regular basis, the pastures would soon be overrun with brush and become worthless for grazing purposes. Roy recalled that when he was a boy there were tramps who went from farm to farm seeking temporary work. Mr. Horton found that tramps from Ireland, where mowing was still done by hand, were very skillful in cutting the pasture brush with a brush scythe, the usual tool employed for this work. Two of these "characters," as Roy called them, Lavin and Sullivan, were often hired by Mr. Horton to do this job. During the few weeks it took to clean up the pastures, they lived in the strawberry pickers' shack. One night they got drunk and somehow set the shack on fire and it burned to the ground. Not knowing for sure just what had happened, Roy remembered the next day watching his father and the hired man John poking in the ashes to see if the two men had burned up in the fire. Since no trace of them was found, it was thought they had escaped unharmed and fearing retribution for destroying the shack, had quickly left town; they were never heard from again.

THE COW

Along the drowsy, dappled lane
An old black cow I see.
She stretches up to scratch her chin
Against an alder-tree.
Her tail flick-flicks the evening flies,
Her tongue, from side to side
Lolls out to taste her leather nose,
All rich with clover made.
Lace-shod in meadowsweet she stands,
Crops buttercup and daisy.
The falling dusk makes no demands,
Her dreams are sweet and easy.
The purple shadows deeper grow,
The night is coming in
To bear away the field, the flower,
The cow, and everything.
But her round eyes are full of peace,
Calm as the summer river.
She only knows that life is this,
And grass goes on for ever.
                    Poem by Pamela Holmes

Drawing by Ann Roper

Chapter IV

FARM ANIMALS

Roy remembered that his father always liked animals and treated them kindly. He never forgot how every evening before going to bed his father would take the lantern and go out to the barn and check on all the animals. Harlan Horton, grandson of Henry W. Horton, recalled seeing his grandfather, almost to the time he died, each evening shuffling out to the barn.

Roy told me of some of his experiences with animals during his boyhood. He had a story to tell of an old mare that worked on the farm for years. Though she injured her hip and could not work, Henry Horton still kept her. He let her do what she wanted and she would wander around the yard and pasture, nibbling and grazing here and there. In back of the house there was an old open cistern, no longer used, that was dug out years before to collect rain water from the roof of the house. Over the cistern was an old mulberry tree on which the horse liked to scratch her back. One day Roy noticed the horse was missing and strange noises were coming from under the mulberry tree. When he checked on it, he found the horse had fallen into the cistern. He ran to find his father who was working somewhere on the farm to tell him what happened. Immediately, Mr. Horton ordered Roy to find Allie Horton to tell him to come right away with his gun to shoot the horse. Allie soon appeared on the scene and performed the disagreeable task. The next day, Roy's father began hauling home loads of gravel and dumping them into the cistern. The horse is still there to this day.

On another occasion, when Roy was a teenager, he himself was called upon to shoot a horse. A man living across the street had come running over, all excited, crying that his horse was down and all done, begging Roy to come over to shoot him to put him out of his misery. Roy had a .22 rifle but did not want to shoot the horse. He really didn't know how. Upon the neighbor's urging he took out his rifle and shot the horse at a mark the owner had laid out with chalk running down the center of the head and across between the eyes. After being shot, the horse never stirred. Roy thought probably he was stunned; he died shortly after.

Another time Roy saw a boar shot. The boar had been domesticated, but for some reason went wild; maybe someone teased him when he was young. No one could get near him. The owner wanted him slaughtered for meat and he did the bloody job with a shotgun.

An unusual incident happened when a Horton cow was let out of her stanchion in the barn to make it easier to have her calf. Baskets of peaches picked from the Horton orchard had been stored temporarily down at the end of the barn in preparation for canning. The cow, having a fondness for peaches, ate them all. The peaches not only gave the cow a bad case of indigestion, but by fermenting in the stomach made her drunk. The Hortons found her staggering around the barn as if she had been out on a binge. She had the calf with no trouble but never gave a drop of milk; Roy remarked that a bad case of bloat always stops the production of milk.

Roy noted that all the Hortons, including his brothers, father, and himself, always preferred a yoke of oxen for the heavy hauling of wood, timber, and manure, instead of horses which in teams or alone were generally used for plowing, cultivating, or mowing because they were faster. As a boy, Roy had the opportunity to work with oxen along with his father who showed him how to manage them. The Hortons preferred the Devon breed of cattle, but at various times they had a pair of Holsteins and even a yoke of Jerseys on the farm. The latter were found, however, to be too "jumpy" to be satisfactory. Roy not only enjoyed working with cattle, but also liked to raise them. One of his last pair, named Barney and Fred, participated in the 1964 tricentennial parade celebrating Taunton's 300th Anniversary. The oxen were yoked to a wagon loaded with an original anchor from the *U.S.S. Constitution* that had been forged in the late eighteenth century at a foundry in the Westville section of Taunton. Roy's son-in-law, Francis

McClellan, who also enjoyed working with oxen, helped Roy with this project. Francis recalled that the oxen had no trouble pulling the heavy anchor in the parade except when trying to get the load started on a hill on Weir Street, Taunton, after the parade had a momentary pause. A truck following the cart came up from behind the cart and gave it a little nudge to get the rig moving again.

Henry Horton kept his oxen in a separate part of the barn from the cows. The oxen were not kept in a stanchion as the cows were; instead, they had a chain around their necks with one end around a vertical pole in such a manner that the end could slide up and down the pole. This arrangement gave the oxen more opportunity for movement and comfort. Since oxen were worked hard, it was felt that their comfort was important.

Roy described for me in detail how oxen were yoked. First the off ox was led out on the barn floor where the yoke was lifted onto the fore part of the shoulder of the ox and a U-shaped wooden bow was slipped up under the neck and fastened with a bow pin. The yoke then was allowed to drop loose around the ox's neck. Next the nigh ox was led out onto the barn floor. The yoke was raised and the ox walked under it. A second wooden bow was slipped up under the neck and fastened with a bow pin. A well trained yoke of oxen would move into their correct position with very little prompting from the driver. The driver, to get his team into motion, would raise his whip and while bringing it down, would call out, "Ha Whoop", and the oxen would start. The oxen then were let out of the barn and led toward the front of the wagon or sled. The off ox would come up to the draw pole from a position along the side of the cart and step over the pole. The driver then slipped the end of the pole through the iron ring hanging below the yoke. The pole was fastened in place by a tapered iron pin called a tongue pin, about three quarters of an inch in diameter. Some yokes had a ring on top for the purpose of hitching on another yoke of oxen for heavy pulling. The driver would walk beside, a little ahead of the nigh ox. The oxen obeyed voice commands, but mostly arm movements. They would also follow the driver. The commands were "Whoa" to stop, "Whoop" or "Come" to start, "Haw" to turn to the left, and "Gee" to turn to the right. Oxen could be

Roy Horton with Salt and Pepper

Raymond Horton

Oxen scenes from the Horton Farm

Load of cord wood heading to the farm

Henry W. Horton guiding his oxen

hitched to a wagon or sled much faster than a team of horses but, compared to horses, they were too slow moving to operate farm implements efficiently.

According to age, oxen were known as yearlings, two year old steers, and three year old steers. They were not called oxen until they were four years old. Up to the time they became oxen they sometimes might be a little difficult to handle, but after they became four years old, they rarely ever gave any trouble. If the oxen were being used only on soft ground, shoes were not needed, but generally shoes were put on, because their feet would wear down too fast on gravel roads or on sharp ice in the winter. Special ice shoes with cleats for gripping were sometimes put on for swamping work.

Roy thought that shoeing the ox was perhaps the hardest thing to do on the farm. A special hoist was made with two wooden cylinders or drums suspended on the hoists of a shed. The Hortons' ox shoeing hoist had been built years ago in a shed behind the house. From these drums two leather straps were attached. The ox was led into the windlass where one belt was put under the front of his body and another under the rear. The drums were then turned so that his weight was barely on the floor. The hoof to be shoed was then tied and lifted off the floor. Other hooves might also be tied, because there would be trouble if the ox kicked and thrashed. Roy recalled that sometimes when working on one hoof, the blacksmith might be kicked in the head by another hoof. The shoe for an ox hoof, being cloved, is unlike a horse shoe. Since the hoof is in two parts, one ox has eight shoes. It is more difficult to drive a nail into an ox hoof, Roy said, because the area of the hoof which can be used is limited. Also, sometimes when the blacksmith had the nail all set to drive, the ox would thrash and upset the work. Once when Roy's father was shoeing two oxen, each of which had a fine pair of horns, each ox knocked off one of his horns from thrashing, leaving them both disfigured. John Simpson of Attleboro, a well known farrier and horse fancier, often did the shoeing of both oxen and horses for the Hortons.

Oxen occasionally may be seen today on New England farms, but mostly they are used at pulling contests at fairs. The modern method of holding the ox while he is being shod is somewhat similar to the winch type hoist used by the Hortons

Present method of shoeing oxen. While the Hortons also placed the ox in a sling, as shown in the picture, today the ox is lifted off the ground hydraulically and rotated on to his side for easy shoeing.

except that hydraulic cylinders are used. Today the ox is led into a metal frame mounted on the back of a truck. Hydraulic cylinders close the frame and hold the ox in position while other cylinders raise the ox off the ground and rotate him horizontally for easy shoeing.

Roy remembered how sometimes when their oxen were old enough and knew their way about the neighborhood, they could be started for home from where the men were working at the end of the day and could be trusted to walk all the way back to the barn unattended. Of course traffic was light then and oxen still being a familiar sight, no one bothered them. The oxen sometimes found their way home after working in Squannakonk Swamp at the end of Maple Lane in Rehoboth. They would walk out the Lane by themselves, turn left on County Street, and continue on that street on to Wellington Street in Dighton to the farm. When they arrived at the farm, the oxen would wait patiently at the barn door until someone appeared to un-yoke them and put them in their stall.

Roy was one of the trustees of the Rehoboth Fair that was founded in 1932 and during later years has been operating at Williams Street in Dighton. One of the main attractions over the last 25 years was the ox pulling contest. While this event was being held, Roy would be sure to be seen sitting in his pick up truck on the edge of the field, viewing the pulling and offering comments to his friends about the quality and ability of the various yokes of cattle. One of the main exhibit buildings has been named the Roy Horton Building to honor Roy's many years of service to the Fair.

Former Fish School, Wellington Street, Dighton. Originally built in 1886, it is now a private residence.

Chapter V

SCHOOLING

Roy's boyhood schools were of the one room variety; consolidation of the schools in Dighton did not begin until the 1920's. Each neighborhood in Dighton had its own school, administered by a school district with all the grades being taught by one teacher. Roy attended the Fish School, named after Abner Fish or his father Daniel Fish, both local residents who had lived at the corner of Smith and Wellington Streets many years earlier. When Roy attended, the school was located about one quarter mile below the farm on the northerly side of Wellington Street. Roy recalled that it was not much of a school when compared to schools today, but it was a lot better than the one his father had attended on the southwest corner of Wellington and Smith Streets, also called the Fish School. In Roy's father's day, schools were always put on street corners for easy access from four directions, but they were also always placed on the poorest land, some place that could not be farmed. The older Fish School was a tiny building perched on the edge of a swamp. If you brought your skates to school, Roy was told by his father, in winter you could put them on in the school and skate out the back door. The first Fish School was built about 1838 and replaced by the newer school in 1886.

Roy related an experience from his school days. One day in 1912, while he was sitting in school, Roy happened to look out the window and saw a herd of about 40 cows meandering down Wellington Street by themselves. Right away, he recognized them as the Horton herd and without saying anything to the teacher, he rushed out the door, grabbed a stick, and managed to turn the lead cows around. With some prodding and chasing after the more stubborn ones, he managed to get them all back through the gate at the lane and back into their pasture. When he returned, the teacher looked astonished, but she gave no rebuke for leaving the class without permission. Thinking about it 75 years later, Roy proudly said that he doubted a kid today would have the presence of mind to do what he did. Not only did he recognize the Horton herd from inside the school, but he never hesitated as to what to do about it.

After the trolley line from Providence to Taunton was constructed through Dighton and Rehoboth in 1899 along Winthrop Street (Route 44), it became possible for school children in both towns to continue their education at Taunton High School. Roy began attending Taunton High School in 1914 and when weather permitted, he rode his bicycle up Wellington Street and New Street in Rehoboth to the corner of New Street and Winthrop Street, known as Wheeler's Corner. He left his bicycle a couple of hundred yards down New Street at the George H. Goff farm before boarding the trolley for the ride into Taunton about eight miles away. Later, Roy's brother Elwood owned this farm. Roy related how a boyhood friend and distant relative, Percy Tinkham, and he attended High School together. Roy said that apparently they were not smart enough or they were too poorly prepared to make the jump from a one room Dighton School to Taunton High School. They struggled along for a few years, but Roy recalled, they didn't know what the teachers were talking about half the time. Finally they gave it up and never graduated. Roy was then seventeen years old. After discussing the situation with his father, Roy was told that there did not seem much of a future for him in farming, that his older brothers Raymond and Elwood were already in it, and since Raymond was beginning to take over the family farm, there was really no room for another son on the farm. Mr. Horton then suggested that Roy learn a trade.

Since Roy liked working with wood and had an interest in carpentry, it was decided he should try to find an established carpenter to take him on as an apprentice. In those days it was difficult to go into carpentry. First it was necessary to find a master carpenter who was willing to take on an apprentice and teach him the trade. Roy did have some self-taught experience from doing shingling and other odd carpentry jobs around the farm. Even so he had a hard time finding a job. Roy always considered himself lucky that Howard Tweedy (1897-1992), an established builder from Taunton, was willing to take him on as an apprentice. Almost the only way to find a carpenter willing to hire an apprentice was to be friendly with someone or to have a relative already established in that vocation. Roy was hired by Mr. Tweedy because Roy's friend Percy Tinkham, who was also looking for a job in that field, had a sister married to Tweedy. Mr. Tweedy had married Percy's sister Bessie M. Tinkham, who persuaded Tweedy to give Percy a job. Mr. Tweedy, being an in-law, had many times visited the Tinkhams at their Smith Street farm where he had met Roy. Apparently he was favorably enough impressed with him to hire him too. Howard Tweedy was then a young man who had entered the trade in similar fashion, completing his apprenticeship under Fairbanks Smith of Taunton, his brother-in-law.

Roy recalled how fortunate they were that Howard Tweedy hired Percy and him for .50 cents per hour, which was later increased to .60 cents. Their first job was assisting Mr. Tweedy to build a house for Milton Minor in Rumford, Rhode Island. Roy recalled that little by little Mr. Tweedy disclosed the secrets of the carpenter's trade to them, not divulging too much at any one time. For example, stair building was an art unknown to them. It was not until Percy and Roy had worked for him a couple of years that Mr. Tweedy showed them some of the tricks of that craft.

After finishing their apprenticeship, Percy and Roy went into business together for four or five years. They always got along very well and had a lot of fun kidding each other on the job. One of the first houses they built by themselves was a house that still stands on the corner of Walker and Winthrop Street, Dighton, for Charles Walker.

In those days only hand tools and the best of material were used; if a finish board had a knot in it, it was discarded. Now, said Roy, everything is used including the old whiney pieces. Apprenticeship with Mr. Tweedy marked the beginning of Roy's career in the carpentry business that was to span 55 years until his retirement in 1973.

Richard K. Witherell House, circa 1900, at the corner of Horton Street and Oak Street, West Dighton. Roy often passed by this house on his way to visit his friend Everett Horton on Winthrop Street, Dighton.

Same view today. The garage was built by Roy in 1965 and the ell was built by Arthur Morton in 1970.

Chapter VI

FRIENDS, NEIGHBORS & CHARACTERS

By the turn of this century, many of the Horton neighbors had lived in the area for all their lives. Many were descended from some of the first settlers of the town. Economic opportunity for all these people was very limited, but some had made the best of a bad situation and by taking advantage of every opportunity that came along, had become comparatively successful, but others had not been as fortunate.

Roy had many friends of his own age. One was Everett Horton who lived about a mile away from the Horton farm if the most difficult but direct route was taken by using short cuts over cart paths and across fields. Roy said that Everett's family was related to his family and lived on Winthrop Street in Dighton at the turn in the road at the top of the road where Brazil's Package Store was located (Buffaloe's Store in 1993). Everett's father was an expert at laying up stone house foundations; he was the best stone mason Roy ever saw. He could put up a cellar wall house foundation waist high in a day for an average size house. There were no ready-mix concrete trucks available then. Stones were taken from old stone walls and brought to the house site by teams of horses. No cement was used. Everett Horton, Sr. had a knack of picking up an irregular stone and finding a place where it would fit in. Roy never could do it. When Roy tried to help, he would pick up a stone, turn it over and over, looking for a place to put it, and then give up and try another. Everett would say disgustedly, "Hey, never pick up a stone and then put it down again. You will never get anywhere doing that." Everett Horton even had a name for certain stones and used to say, "Give me that Old Doxology or hand me old Methuselah."

When Roy wanted to visit at the Horton house, he would

take a short cut rather than go by the roads. He would cut across his grandfather James Horton's farm, pass down by the Old Slough, and if there was ice, walk down the brook and out to Oak Street. A little way down Oak Street at what is now Mr. Jesse's land he turned left on his lane, which came out at a corner of the old Elder Goff farm, now the present Dighton-Rehoboth Regional High School athletic field. Here he turned right and took a path across the Pedro Baptist Church Ministerial land to Maple Swamp Road. From there he went on a nice path through the woods that led up to the rear of Everett's house. Roy remembered that a little south of his friend's house there was an interesting rock formation called the Wolf's Den that the boys liked to explore. This was a natural cave in the rock and it went quite a way in.

Another friend of Roy, although of another generation, was the hired man, John Stanley. Roy always spoke fondly of him and of the many hours they spent laboring together on the farm. John's last name was Figurado, but for some reason he had it changed to Stanley. He came to work on the farm as a young man when Roy's brother Raymond was three years old, reminisced Roy, and stayed until he was age 77. John had come from Portugal at age 16 and moved right away on to the Horton farm as a hired man. About the same time, the Hortons hired Bertha, a young immigrant woman from Canada, to help with the housekeeping. It was not long before John and Bertha were married and moved to a small house down the street from the farm that Roy's father rented to them. John continued to work on the farm and over the years became a most trusted employee. Mr. Horton paid him $17.00 per week and farm produce; in return John worked very hard, seven days a week. Roy's nephew, Harlan, recalled that once when everyone on the farm was attending the annual 4th of July clam bake at the West Dighton Church, he saw John drive by in the farm wagon with a cultivator on the back heading for the field at "Shubaels" on Winfield Lane to cultivate corn. No one asked him to do this task on a holiday; he did it of his own accord. John was treated like a member of the family and according to Roy, he was not shy about bossing his father around when he saw things that needed to be done on the farm. Each morning John came early to the Horton house for breakfast where he sat around the table with the Horton family discussing with them what work needed to be done that day.

Emeline Chace was a neighbor who lived on a farm at the corner of Hornbine Road and Simmons Street in Rehoboth where in 1986 Tony Gonsalves was living. Roy said it was a beautiful place with a small well kept house and beautiful stone walls. Later owners neglected the grounds somewhat, but when Emeline lived there it was neat as a pin. Roy thought she was not married and living off the farm income and a small inheritance she had received from her father. Roy remembered that when he was about seven or eight (1907), on a Sunday afternoon his father asked him if he wanted to go with him to see Mrs. Chace about buying some spiles (oak trees used for bridge and dock piles) from her woods that he needed to fill a contract for the repair of the Dighton - Berkley bridge. Since Roy was always willing for an excuse to get away from the farm, he immediately agreed to go and went out to help his father harness the horse to the democrat wagon. After arriving at the Chace farm, Roy sat outside on the wagon parked in the dooryard, while his father went inside to talk. He still could recall how attractive the grounds were and how well the house and farm buildings were kept up. After about a half an hour visit, Mr. Horton came out and Roy heard Mrs. Chace say, "Take all the white oak you want, Henry, and pay me what it is worth. I trust you to do right by me." Later he accompanied his father when he was getting out those logs over the lane leading into Manwhague Swamp, near the present Everett Gonsalves house.

Not all the neighbors however were that friendly with the Hortons; one family in particular Roy remembered. This family lived nearby in the vicinity of Smith Street and Wellington Street. Once Roy's father and John the hired man had raised some potatoes on the Manchester Lot on Smith Street. In the fall the task of digging out and bagging the potatoes was begun. The bags were finally filled, but because it was getting late in the day and cows had to be milked, they were left on the edge of the field for carting home the next morning. When Henry Horton and John drove up in the wagon the next day, all the potatoes were gone. Henry looked angry, but said only "we shall see." He went immediately down to the house of the neighbor whom he suspected of stealing the potatoes and saw the father and son working in the yard. Driving up to the son, who had a bad reputation, Henry demanded the return of the potatoes. The son denied knowing anything about them. Henry then replied sternly, "I want them back or I will get someone to make you do it." He then left. The next day when Henry and John visited the field all the potatoes were back, just where he had left them. Roy added that the son of this family was no good and that the father was just the opposite. Probably it was the son who was solely responsible for the theft. He was not beyond stealing even from his own father. Once he took a load of his father's wood into Providence and sold it. Instead of returning home he spent the wood money on a ticket to Block Island for himself and a girl he had just met. On the Island he spent the rest of the money and he could not get back to the mainland; so he stole the girl's jewelry, hawked it, and used the money for a ticket home. Still his father always trusted him.

At the turn of the century there were a number of people in town who were known as characters. These individuals had lived in the area all their lives and were descended from families who had been there for generations. In many cases the later generation was no better off than their ancestors had been. Because of a lack of education or lack of business opportunities, many of these people had just given up trying to improve themselves economically and would do as little work as possible. In many cases they were perfectly satisfied with the way things were. The economy then, however, was such that a person could get along with very little. By picking up odd jobs here and there and working a little on their small farms they were able to get by. Many supplemented their income by hunting and trapping. According to Roy these characters often drank too much hard cider which was plentiful and easy to make, but never got really drunk, just "boozy." Sometimes these characters were called "run out yankees." In contrast, people who were industrious and had good work habits were according to Roy, often referred to as "coming from good stock," as if they were being compared to cattle at an auction.

There could not have been more of a contrast than between Emeline Chace living at her neat little farm on Simmons Street and her relatives Barney and Albert Chace who lived farther up the road at the corner of Simmons Street and Cedar Street on part of the present Vandenberg farm. They were as different as day and night. Roy often used to see the Chace brothers when the Hortons pastured dry cows in their pasture during the summer and in the fall when the brothers would help Roy's father husk corn. The Chaces could not read or write and did not seem to care. They lived by hunting and a few odd jobs. They knew how to catch a fox and where to sell its hide. They were dirty, uncouth, and shiftless. When they earned $1.00 it went a long way. They would walk to Taunton for liquor but when they had money they rode the trolley. When on the trolley, they talked loud and would stare at someone and say, "I know you," much to that person's embarrassment. One story Roy told about the Chaces was how they decided to count their hens. Albert would shove them out of the little hen door while Barney on the outside counted them exiting. He began, "one, two, three;" then after a long pause, Barney went around to the big door of the hen house and yelled into Albert, "Hell of a lot of them ain't there, Albert." He could not count any further. Only the ruins from these past activities are to be seen now and the farm has grown back into brush and trees; a cellar hole presently remains where the Chace house stood.

 Roy went on to describe another familiar neighbor, also considered to be a character, a farmer over in Rehoboth. He ran a small dairy farm and wood business, but did not amount to very much. He was nothing like his neighbors, David W. Francis and Francis J. Wheeler, who were very successful in both of these business activities. Oysters were very common then in Narragansett Bay before pollution and hurricanes devastated the oyster beds. After delivering a load of wood or some vegetable crop in Providence, it was common for a farmer to take some of the profit to buy oysters to bring home with him from one of the numerous oyster houses. This neighbor loved oysters and was known for his eating capacity. Roy recalled that when he went to an Oyster Supper at the West Dighton Church, that neighbor could eat as many as ten men. When Roy's father wanted to buy oysters in Providence, he brought a container shaped like a small milk can along to carry them home in. On one trip, after delivering vegetables at the market, he had the can filled with oysters at one of the oyster houses. Later, while travelling home towards Dighton, somewhere on Taunton Avenue in Seekonk he caught up with this oyster loving neighbor. As was the custom, the neighbor climbed up on the Horton wagon after tieing his rig behind. As they ambled along talking about various things, the neighbor, after remarking on the nice oysters Henry had, began dipping in the can for a tender morsel. Mr. Horton never said anything, but after they each parted for his own farm, he found the neighbor had eaten over half his oysters.

Roy reported another story that went around about this neighbor. Everyone knew that this man watered his milk, a fairly common practice in those days. He always had a few characters hanging around the farm helping him with this and that. One day they decided to play a joke on him after the neighbor had told them he was going to be away until evening. Before leaving he directed them to feed his cows by giving the most corn stalks to the cows producing the most milk, a less amount to the next smaller producer, and so on down through the herd. When he came home later, he saw the corn piled all around the well. When he went into the barn to ask the men what the corn was doing at the well, they replied, "you said give the most corn to the biggest producer."

Another neighbor, also a character, was Stephen H. Davis (1843-1922) who lived at the George H. Goff farm, then being run by George's son, Arthur Goff, near the corner of Winthrop Street and New Street in Rehoboth. Mr. Davis was a widower who for most of his life had lived on his father's farm at 225 Anawan Street, Rehoboth. Here he raised a family and generally worked on the farm for his father, Deacon John Davis, Jr. (1813-1883). Deacon John was a prominent and successful farmer and wood and charcoal dealer. After helping to found the Anawan Union Baptist Church in 1840, for the rest of his life he was always known as "Deacon" and was considered very religious. Being also community minded, in 1875 he donated a lot from his farm to build the Anawan School, a one room school house which is now in the home of Nancy Fuller at 222 Anawan Street. The original Anawan School, dating from the mid 18th century had stood at the corner of Anawan Street and Fairview Avenue. Besides operating a very successful dairy farm, Deacon John also prospered in the wood and charcoal business. If Roy had known him I am sure he would have classified him as one of Rehoboth's Wood Operators, similar to those he knew in later years living on New Street. (See Chapter V, Wood Operators). Deacon John died in 1883 after a long illness which left his estate almost penniless, and forced his children to sell his farm.

His son Stephen was also a farmer, but unlike his father, was never much of a success in that field or in the wood and charcoal business either. Like so many at that time, Stephen did just about enough work here and there to get by. When Roy knew Stephen he was living with his daughter, Isabelle Goff, wife of Arthur H. Goff at the Goff farm on New Street and was being cared for by them during his old age. Stephen lived downstairs and the Goff family lived upstairs in the Goff house.

Steve Davis as he was called was known for his fiddling ability. When the young people in the neighborhood decided to have a dance, sometimes at the Hall across the street from the Hortons' Wellington Street home in Dighton or at the Anawan Inn at Winthrop Street, Rehoboth, they often asked Steve to play. Roy remembered that if you gave him something to drink, usually hard cider, he would fiddle all evening for free. Pearl Wheeler Quint, who was a few years younger than Roy, does not remember Mr. Davis playing at dances, but does remember that when the neighborhood children would see him out in the front yard, they would ask him to get his fiddle and play. With very little urging, he would go into the house, return with the fiddle, and play any music they wanted. Pearl recalled that he played very well.

Roy often saw Mr. Davis when he left his bicycle at the Goff farm while taking the trolley to high school in Taunton. World War I was raging at the time in France and the president, Woodrow Wilson, a Democrat, had a law passed creating War Time. It was the same as Day Light Saving Time today only it was in force year-round. It was the first time that clocks had been set ahead to lengthen the daylight into the evening. Many of the old Yankee farmers, particularly Republicans, did not like the change; one of them was Stephen H. Davis. Sometimes as Roy would pull up at the Goff yard on his bicycle, he would yell over to Mr. Davis to ask him what time it was, to hear how much time he had before catching the trolley to Taunton. Steve Davis would reply, "Do you want God's time or God Damn Wilson's time?"

Anawan Inn, circa 1910, at the corner of Winthrop Street and Anawan Street Rehoboth, where Steve Davis fiddled at dances.

The same corner today

Chapter VII

LATER YEARS

Roy's oldest brother Elwood was the first to leave the farm. First he lived on Horton Street in Dighton across from the old Goff Meeting House, where he began to farm for himself. Later about 1930, after Arthur H. Goff died, Elwood bought the George Hathaway Goff farm on New Street in Rehoboth. Here with his son Lyman he operated a dairy farm well into his seventies and almost to the day he died in 1964. His death occurred when he was working up in his hay mow where either by accident or from a stroke, he fell out the door and died shortly after.

The second oldest son Raymond remained at the Wellington Street Horton homestead and continued to farm jointly with his father for a number of years. An addition was put on the old Paul farmhouse; Raymond and his family lived in one part while Henry and Hannah lived in the other section. Because of old age, Henry began taking a less active role in operating the farm, while Raymond's son Harlan, as he matured, became more actively involved in running the farm with his father. Roy once said that all the Hortons if they lived long enough ended up with knee problems. Henry was to be crippled with his affliction and Roy also suffered greatly from bad knees for the last fifteen or twenty years of his life. By the middle 1950's Harlan had taken over most of the farm work and his father had been reduced because of ill health to doing the menial jobs, like caring for the calves and doing some of the paper work. Harlan recalled that when he was a boy during the 1930's, he used to see his grandfather Henry doing the less strenuous work while Raymond did the heavy farm work. Henry's wife Hannah died in 1942 and Henry died from a stroke a few months later in 1943.

Raymond and Harlan found that by the 1950's the economics of dairy farming had drastically changed. Because of improved transportation, milk from farms in Vermont, New York State, and other far off places could be shipped into eastern Massachusetts economically. These farms were large, had good soil and few rocks, and thus could be run efficiently with modern motorized farm equipment. Many of these farms had milking herds of up to 100 cows and dairy equipment that pumped the milk directly from the cow through a special pipe line into a large holding tank. The Hortons were continuing to handle the milk by the old method of pouring it by hand from each cow into 40 quart cans. The cans were still delivered each morning to the dairy as before, but by pick-up truck, rather than by the democrat wagon. The old method was not only less sanitary than the new procedure, but it was also more labor intensive; the 40 quart milk cans then in use were heavy to handle. The Hortons had arranged the old barn so that it could be filled with cows to its capacity. A string of cows was held in stanchions on each side of the barn and one string across the rear, making room for a total of about 35 cows, hardly enough to be competitive with the out of state herds of three times that size.

The end came to this old fashioned layout when the dairy wholesaler no longer would accept milk delivered to his dairy in the 40 quart cans, but insisted that his specially built milk tank truck be sent to the farm to pick up the milk. Since the milk pickup had to be every other day in order to save the wholesaler labor and travel costs, the Hortons had to purchase a special tank called a bulk milk tank. This tank was specially designed out of stainless steel and refrigerated; it was an expensive item for a farmer with a small herd to own. To make matters worse it was hardly economical for the wholesaler to send the big milk tank truck to the Horton farm for the milk from just 35 cows. Harlan and Raymond were forced like all the other small dairy farmers in Rehoboth and Dighton at that time to make a choice of either greatly expanding their operation or going out of business. Many small dairies took the second choice, but the Hortons decided to take the plunge and go into a large scale operation.

The old Horton dairy barn was remodeled into a combination storage area for cows' bedding and a tractor garage. About 30 feet to the south of the old barn, in the area where Henry W.

Horton used to build his hay stacks for extra feed during the winter, a barn 160 feet long and 40 feet wide was built. Later a 30 foot addition was added, giving the building a total length of 190 feet. Roy, with his carpenters, was engaged to do the construction work. The walls were laid up with cement blocks on which Roy and his men built a huge truss roof under which bales of hay could be stored. To save money the roof timbers were all sawed out of old telephone poles and pilings at the Gustafson saw mill on Winthrop Street in Dighton. Harlan remembered that when he was helping with the roof timbers, he became badly burned from the creosote in the old wood. He commented that it was awful stuff to work with. Again to save money, rather that build an upright silo, an old building foundation was converted near the farm into a pit type silo. In 1959, the work was completed and 130 cows were purchased of which about 86 were milked at one time. the others being dry until the birth of their next calf. Since each new cow cost $600 to $700 dollars each, this was another large investment. The purchase was made through a cattle dealer who agreed to hold the mortgage on the cows. A new 800 gallon bulk milk tank was installed with a pipe line milking system. On the plus side, the new cows produced so much more milk that the bulk tank was filled sooner than the two day pickup schedule required and the old 40 quart milk cans sometimes still had to be used to store the extra milk.

The Hortons lacked enough farm fields to feed this number of cows, and even if they had, it would be doubtful that the rocky land would grow the quality feed required to maintain a high milk output. Consequently, a new kind of hay was bought through a hay broker in Easton, Massachusetts, and trucked to the farm from Wellington, Vermont. This hay was called Birdsfoot Trefoil and the cows loved it. Its legacy can still be seen growing on the shoulders of Wellington Street; when a hay truck was leaving the farm some of the seed would blow off, sprout, take root, and now it comes up each year. Trefoil has a small yellow flower when it blooms. Corn was also no longer grown on the farm. Arrangements were made with Hyman Fine of Smith Street in Attleboro, the largest sweet corn grower in the area at that time, to buy his corn stalks after the corn had been picked. The stalks were harvested with a corn chopper, blown into a truck, and stored in the ground silo at the farm.

This type of farm operation was altogether different from the general style farm that had been begun back in Harlan's great grandfather's day. While the general farm was run almost entirely in harmony with nature, returning all the fertility that was taken from the soil, the new farm was more similar to a factory operation; no feed for the cows was raised on the farm and no manure was returned to the soil. Similar to operating a factory, the Hortons purchased all the grain and hay (raw materials) for the cows (the machines) and sold the milk (finished product) to a wholesaler or middleman. Since that number of cows generated so much manure, disposing of it could have created a problem. Fortunately there were still a large number of truck garden farms operating in Dighton and neighboring Swansea that were able to utilize all the manure the farm produced; disposing of it never became a problem. In contrast the old general farm had been operated on almost a closed system with only grain and some commercial fertilizer being purchased. All the other forage was grown on the farm and all manure was returned to the soil to fertilize the next crop. No longer on the new farm was there time or was it economically feasible to carry on former farm practices like swamping, tending an orchard, looking after a yoke of oxen, or raising vegetables.

The Hortons, now having so many cows to milk each day, seven days a week, had a very rigid schedule to follow. Harlan recalled that all the work to manage this large herd was done by himself and one hired man, Francis McClellan, Roy's son-in-law. By this time, his father had had a heart attack and was not able to do anything but light work. The Hortons' new schedule was very intense and went, according to Harlan, something like this: Harlan began the day's work in the barn at 4:00 in the morning. First he fed grain to all the cows to get them up. While they were eating, he scraped their platforms and began cleaning the gutters with the manure conveyor. Next, he brushed the spilled grain back into the mangers, threw down the hay from the mow above, and began milking. After the milking with a machine was finished and the equipment washed out, he would load a cart with sawdust and with a tractor pull it into the barn. The sawdust was used to bed down the cows. Since the cows stayed in the barn 24 hours a day, the Horton pastures were no longer needed and began to grow up in brush. This work usually took until 7:30 A.M. at which time Harlan went home for breakfast. After breakfast, he brushed back the hay into the mangers and took the tractor and cart to the silage pit, loaded it up, and fed the silage to the cows. For the rest of the day there were calves to tend to, cows to breed, equipment to be maintained, and errands to run. At 4:00 P.M. the whole procedure began again, except that no silage was fed in the evening, only hay and grain. Francis McClellan, who helped Harlan with this work, remembered that Harlan had two days off a week, Thursday and Saturday. On Sunday the two men just did the chores, *i.e.,* milking and feeding the cows. There was no vacation or holiday time for either of the two.

Harlan added that even though the soil was too rocky and the fields too small to raise the amount of feed needed for that number of cows, he, like his grandfather, did have one advantage over the New York and Vermont farms. Their proximity to the large nearby city markets always offered them a place to sell farm produce.

One night in May, 1964, 100 years of dairying on the Horton farm came to a catastrophic end. Raymond had gone out for the evening to attend a farm meeting at the Bristol County Agricultural School. Harlan as usual had gone to bed about 9:00 P.M. because he had to get up early in the morning to begin the chores. Raymond came home at 11:00 P.M. and as was the custom, he, as the last person to bed, walked through the barn to see if everything was secure. Seeing nothing amiss, he went into the dairy room and sat down for a while with his two dogs when suddenly he smelled smoke. When he saw heavy smoke beginning to appear down at the end of the barn near the manure conveyor, he rushed into the house calling to Harlan upstairs for help. Harlan appeared as rapidly as possible, rushed into the barn which by this time was filling with smoke, and tried to release the cows from the stanchions. Francis McClellan, who was living in the old James H. Horton home next to the farm, heard the commotion and woke up to see the flames coming through the barn roof. As he approached the barn he saw Harlan staggering out yelling, "They are all dead, don't go in there. If I did not know my way around in there, I would not have been able to find my way out." Harlan later said that when he was in the barn the smoke was billowing around the cows in acrid clouds and that the cows all had died from the thick smoke and not the flames.

When the Dighton Fire Department was notified of the fire, before leaving the station the chief looked over toward West Dighton and could see the sky was red. Right away knowing this was more than his Department could handle, he called the Rehoboth Fire Department for assistance. Both Fire Departments were hampered in their efforts from a lack of water, there being no water mains on this part of Wellington Street. When the tank on the fire truck was empty, it was necessary to leave the fire scene and refill the tank at the nearest water hole. When the Rehoboth Fire Department arrived, Francis told them to pump out of the well in the back of the house. The firemen scoffed at the idea, saying their big pump would pump that well out in less than a minute. At Francis's urging and despite their misgivings, they gave it a try and hooked their pumper up to the well; they never pumped it dry. Francis said it was an excellent well that had the capacity to provide water for three houses and all the water needed for over 100 cows, including their drinking and wash water. The water from this well was sprayed on to the Horton house and old barn. Francis feels this action is about all that saved them both from going up in flames; a light wind blowing away from the house also helped. Even so, the old barn shingles were smoking so badly that it looked to Francis as if the barn was about to explode; if that had happened nothing could have saved the house. Wind blown embers also sailed across the road and set a field on fire.

The next day what had been a thriving dairy business was nothing but a pile of ashes. All that had been saved were about 30 head of young cattle who had been out in the barn yard getting accustomed to going to pasture over at the old Tinkham Farm. Ninety cows died and all the milking equipment and a farm tractor were lost. The total loss was figured to be over $100,000.00. Ten pieces of fire equipment were at the scene, seven from Dighton and three from Rehoboth. Upon inspection when the embers cooled, it was thought that the fire had begun in the manure conveyor motor. Raymond thought of starting up again and rebuilding and even took out a construction permit. It did not go any further then that because Raymond was not well. The loss was traumatic to both Hortons and probably it hastened Raymond's death a year later. Today all that remains of the Horton dairy barn are the foundation ruins. The site is now a pasture for a couple of beef cows. Much of the rest of the farm is now a housing development. The old Paul-Horton barn still stands, and has recently been rebuilt by the present owner, Thomas Horton, to board riding horses.

END OF A DAIRY BUSINESS —All that remains today of a thriving dairy business in Dighton are the cinder blocks that only yesterday formed a barn housing a herd of 90 milking cows. All the animals perished in the blaze which was out of control when firefighters arrived. (*Gazette* Photo and Caption, May 6, 1964)

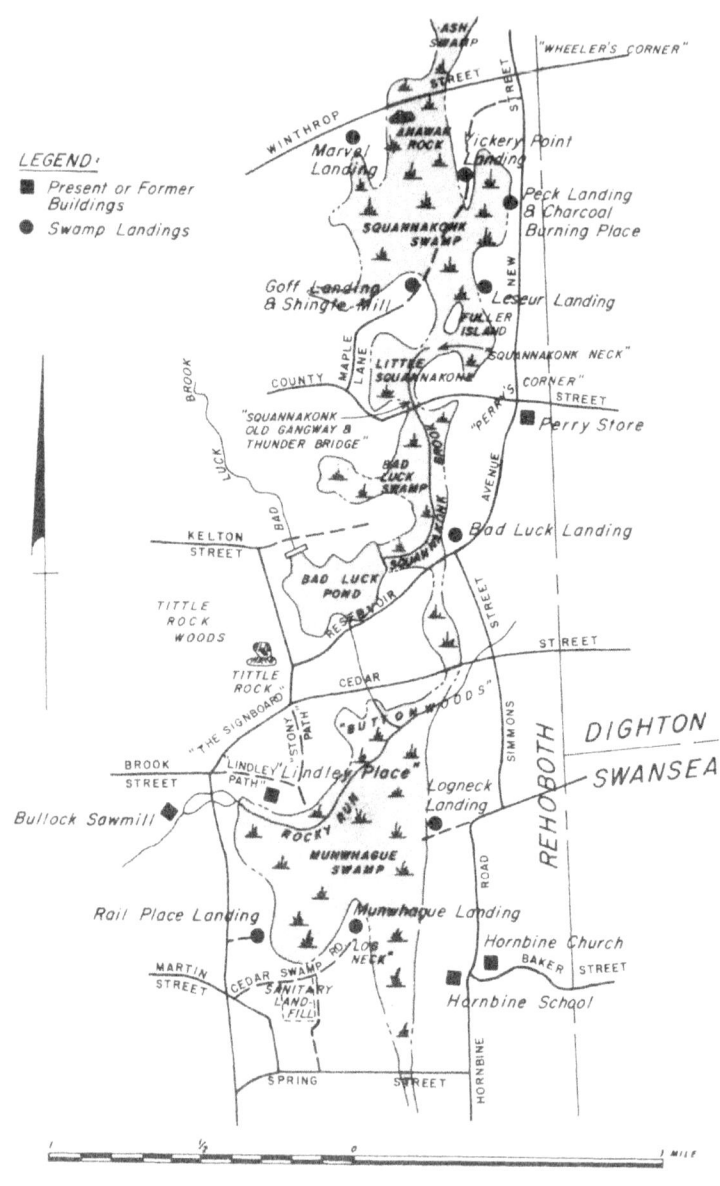

SWAMPS AND LANDINGS
Rehoboth, circa 1900

PART 2

ROY W. HORTON, SWAMPER

The only place where I feel the eminent domain is in my wood lot. My spirits rise whenever I enter it. I can spend the entire day there with hatchet or pruning shears making paths, without a remorse of wasting time. I fancy the birds know me, and even the trees make little speeches or hint them.
                              Ralph Waldo Emerson

Circa 1925, Fred M. Smith of North Rehoboth hauling white cedar poles to the oyster companies on Narragansett Bay, Rhode Island. These poles had been cut in the Great Cedar Swamp (Seekonk Cedar Swamp) North Rehoboth.

Chapter I

SWAMPS

Although dairy farming and raising vegetables were important sources of the Horton family income, the sale of firewood and timber was of equal significance. During the spring, summer, and early fall, the Hortons were mainly occupied with such general farm activities as plowing, planting, haying, cultivating and harvesting the vegetables and corn crops. The rest of the year, Mr. Horton and his hired men were in the woods cutting and hauling out cords of firewood and tons of timber in conjunction with his wood business. Most of this woodcutting took place in the swamps in the easterly part of Rehoboth or on the upland woodlots in westerly Dighton. Buying woodlots to keep the business supplied with sufficient cordwood and timber was also crucial to the family economy.

When the Rehoboth swamps — Squannakonk, Bad Luck, and Manwhague — are visited today, it is nearly impossible to visualize how extensively they were once used and how impressive were the profits made from them by the nineteenth century "wood operators," as Roy liked to call these fellow Swamp Yankees. Once it is understood how vital these swamps were to the local economy in the eighteenth, nineteenth, and even into the early twentieth centuries, it is logical that the swamp workers came to be known as Swamp Yankees. Not only were their farms close to the swamps, but they also spent many months of the year working in them. Newcomers from the hilly inland towns of Massachusetts and Rhode Island were no doubt surprised to discover how important the swamps of southeastern Massachusetts were to the local farmers and how much they were utilized.

From the earliest days of the settlement of West Dighton and the easterly part of Rehoboth to the early decades of the twentieth century, the Squannakonk, Manwhague, and Bad Luck Swamps in East Rehoboth played a major part in the economy of the area. Of the three swamps, Squannakonk Swamp has the most historical significance. The Indian chief Anawan was captured at the north end of the Swamp by the English settlers in 1676, thus ending King Philip's War. The names Squannakonk and Manwhague originated with the Indians and their meanings are now lost. It is also not known how Bad Luck Swamp got its name. According to old records the general area was called Bad Luck before any settlement took place here.

Manwhague Swamp, the largest of the three, contains about 900 acres and is situated toward the southern part of Rehoboth. This Swamp lies west of Hornbine Road, east of Plain Street, north of Spring Street, and its northern border touches the southern end of Bad Luck Swamp at Cedar Street. When the Hortons travelled to this Swamp from their farm on Wellington Street, they approached the Swamp from the north on the old cart path that begins at the corner of Gorham and Plain Streets in Rehoboth, known to the Hortons as the Sign Board Corner. This path to the Swamp, known as the Stony Path, crossed land owned by George and Warren Holden, went over another path called the Lindley Path, and reached the northern border of the Swamp east of the present Moe Horton house on Plain Street. Roy noted that there were other approaches to the Swamp: farmers coming from the east side of the Swamp entered from the lane running west from the sharp bend in Hornbine Road; farmers living near Spring Street entered either from a path that began near the Plain Street four corners and ran easterly by the present Rehoboth land fill to a peninsula jutting into the Swamp known as Log Neck or from a path leading north from Spring Street that intersected the last mentioned path near Log Neck. The Lindley Path, another well travelled path to the Swamp, began near the corner of Brook Street and Plain Street and ran east to intersect the Stony Path. The Lindley Path was named after Lindley Horton who once had a house far off the public road near the intersection of the two paths.

Landings, where logs and timber were drawn out of the Swamp to the upland and loaded on to wagons, were located at the ends of each of these paths. Deep wagon ruts can still be seen on the Log Neck Path, an indication of the heavy wagon and sled traffic that once took place there. Another popular landing was off the easterly side of Plain Street on land now owned by Nathalie Merchant. This landing was known either as Thrasher's Landing or the Rail Place. The latter name indicates that cedar trees were once drawn out here and split into fence rails for use on the neighboring farms.

Bad Luck Swamp, the next swamp to the north, contains about 200 acres and was the smallest of the three. This Swamp is located west of Reservoir Avenue and touched the south end of Squannakonk Swamp at County Street at a place known in the early days of the town by the unusual name of Squannakonk Old Gangway. The Old Gangway is now County Street. The major landing for Bad Luck Swamp was on the northwest side of Reservoir Avenue about opposite Simmons Street on land now owned by Anthony Belcher. This is the landing that the Hortons most often used.

Squannakonk Swamp with about 800 acres is almost as large as Manwhague. This Swamp lies west of New Street, north of Bad Luck Swamp at County Street, and it touches the south end of the Ash Swamp at Winthrop Street (Route 44). The Swamp had several landings on the west side of New Street on property once owned by David W. Francis and Francis J. Wheeler. Other landings were at the end of Sheldon Lane and on land presently owned by Vincent Cavallaro. The most popular landing was located in the heart of the Swamp on a peninsula called Squannakonk Neck at Maple Lane. This was the landing generally used by the Hortons. Other landings were off the southern tip of Vickery Point, a peninsula jutting into the northerly end of the Swamp, and on another peninsula on the former Marvel land at the northwest corner of the Swamp, west of Vickery Point. From these last three landings well worn paths led out to the nearest streets, sections of which can still be seen today.

During the eighteenth and nineteenth centuries the forest products growing in these three swamps were very important to the local farmers. The swamps provided white cedar for shingles, fence rails for the farms, oyster poles for oyster fishermen in Narragansett Bay, hardwoods for timber, spiles, firewood, and charcoal, and white pine for lumber. When the cold weather arrived and the swamps froze up, Roy remembered that men from all directions showed up in the swamps to begin their yearly cutting of stove wood and timber for themselves or for sale. The chop of the ax could be heard all over the swamp as people harvested their wood. Some did their own chopping but others like Ellery Goff of Rehoboth Village and Henry W. Horton hired wood cutters for that purpose. Mr. Horton did his own sledding, but Mr. Goff hired out that work as well.

Many swamp lots that had originally been laid out to normal size had been divided and redivided within a family over several generations, creating some unusual lot shapes. In one case, an original owner owned a long rectangular tract of twenty acres in Manwhague Swamp a little north of Log Neck. After passing through several generations of the family the lot had been divided again and again until some parcels were only 33 feet wide by a half a mile long. It now defies the imagination to see how an owner of one of these lots could cut the wood and cedar on his sliver of swamp without wandering off on to his neighbor's lot, especially in view of the rough terrain and poor land surveys of that time. Family determination to keep possession of swamp lots is an indication of how important they had become to a farmer as a source of fence rails before the invention of barbed wire in the 1880's.

Even though the swamps had furnished large quantities of firewood, cedar, and timber during the first two centuries, there were still large amounts of pine, white cedar, maple, and other hardwoods growing there up to the late 1800's. This was because of the short time that wood could be harvested each year. There were only a few months of the year when the ice was thick enough to support the workmen, horses, and oxen. After the Civil War, when firewood became very profitable to sell in the nearby cities, more enterprising farmers began a concerted action to harvest the trees in the swamps. Gangs of men, yokes of oxen, and teams of horses were organized on a large scale and quantities of cedar and hardwoods were removed. During this period several neighborhood farmers made small fortunes by dealing in these wood products. In one case, a wood cutter from Fall River, Joseph Lunan, in 1910 set up a narrow gauge light weight gas driven railroad in Manwhague Swamp and began hauling out a rich harvest of cedar and white pine to the portable saw mill he had erected at a landing on the shore of the swamp. The use of a railroad permitted him to haul wood from the swamp independent of ice conditions. (Additional railroad information, page 97)

Old Rehoboth records indicate that these swamps were covered with an ancient growth of white cedar and were invariably referred to as Squannakonk Cedar Swamp and Manwhague Cedar Swamp. Bad Luck Swamp apparently never had as heavy a growth of cedar and the word *cedar* was never associated with it*. The white cedar had gotten its start thousands of years ago from the cool climate in this area associated with the retreating glacier. The cedar, liking colder weather, could continue to grow as the climate became milder because the evaporation of the water in the swamps protected by a shaded canopy overhead created the required cool temperatures for the cedar to thrive during the summer. The heavy logging that occurred in the late 1800's and early 1900's removed most of the white cedar, and with the loss of that protective cover, the remaining cedars had trouble reseeding themselves and eventually were replaced by the prolific red or swamp maple. Today the maple tree is the dominant species, although occasional stands of cedar are still to be found and the white pine is plentiful in places. This swamp mixture of white pine, white cedar, and red maple was familiar to Roy when he was young.

Roy noted that many of the landmarks in the swamp were named after some topographic feature or after an early owner in the area. Vickery Point, named after the Vickery family, was a long peninsula in the north end of Squannakonk Swamp that extended southerly into the swamp; Fuller's Island was a three acre island in the same Swamp east of the end of Maple Lane and named after the Fuller family that once owned it;

---

* An excellent but small stand of cedar was cut in the swamp about 1898 along Squannakonk Brook where it enters Bad Luck Pond to build a log club house for the Anawan Club, a privately owned sportsmen's club. Thomas Violette, an experienced hunter and woodsman, was brought down from Maine to supervise the cutting of the cedar and the building of the log cabin. After the clubhouse was completed, Mr. Violette was employed as steward by the club for many years.

Squannakonk Neck was the peninsula running into the same Swamp north from County Street where Maple Lane is now located; Chestnut Island is between Squannakonk Swamp and Bad Luck Swamp where the two met at County Streets. Other lots within a swamp had been named years ago after an early lot owner or after some other features to make them more recognizable, such as Ministerial Swamp, once owned by the Rehoboth Congregational Church, from which cedar and wood were sold to help support the minister. Other names were Maxwell Swamp, Peck Swamp, Bliss Swamp, Carpenter Swamp, Abigail Moulton Swamp, and Bellanger Swamp, all old family names in Rehoboth. Manwhague Swamp contained Daniel Carpenter Swamp, Moulton Swamp named after two eccentric brothers George N. and John B. Moulton who owned large tracts of land in Rehoboth, Martin Swamp near Log Neck, and Ninety-two Rod Swamp that was 92 rods (1/4 mile) long and a few rods (33 feet) wide. Bad Luck Swamp had other names such as Goff Swamp, Horton Swamp, McCormick Swamp, and the Sprague Lot.

Chapter II

SWAMPING

After the harvest at the farm was completed and the swamps had filled up with water from the fall rains, the Hortons would wait with anticipation for the first real freeze which usually occurred about the first of January. When the ice became thick enough to support a yoke of oxen and a sled, Roy's father would announce to his sons that it was time to get some "pine out." This process was called *pining out* because after the pine had been cut, it had to be sledded on the ice out of the swamp right away to one of the landings on the upland before a thaw came. Although snow and ice in the swamp made the best sledding conditions, Roy said that sometimes they were still able to draw out wood even when the ground was bare; the sled would slide fairly easily on the wet swamp grass and frozen grass tufts and high spots. However, sledding without ice was avoided if possible because, if a soft spot in the swamp was encountered, the cattle or horses could get mired down and into considerable difficulty or the load would tip off if the ground gave way under one side of the sled. Ralph Horton (1899-1984), who was brought up on a dairy farm in Rehoboth Village, recalled hearing how his great-grandfather George L. Horton and his grandfather George H. Horton in 1880 drove their yoke of oxen and sled over a path that is on the present Karl Drown farm from County Street to their lot in Bad Luck Swamp. On the way out the oxen and the loaded sled struck a soft spot and became so mired into the mud that the load of wood had to be thrown off and left behind. They were so discouraged by that experience they never went back again.

It was often difficult to determine who the owners of the swamp lots were and even more difficult to locate some of the old lot corners. Most of these boundary locations had been passed down orally from father to son over several generations. The Hortons worked them out as best they could by locating old cedar stakes, blazed trees, or an occasional field stone bound that some farmer years ago had hauled into the swamp to mark his lot corner. Sometimes it helped to ask for help from some of the old families that lived on the borders of the swamp. There was always the fear that wood and timber would be cut on the wrong lot with consequent difficulties with neighbors. Even when an old survey plan was available, it sometimes was inaccurate. In one case in 1830 the Rehoboth Congregational Church engaged a surveyor to run the lines of the Ministerial Swamp in the heart of Squannakonk Swamp. When finished, the surveyor wrote an interesting observation at the bottom of the plan, "I surveyed this land according to the instructions of the church committee, but I do not think it is correct." If the surveyor in 1830 was having trouble locating lot corners at a time when the original land divisions were fairly new and many original corners still existed, it is not difficult to imagine the trouble the Hortons were having in the same area 75 years later.

Roy related how his father hired woodcutters to chop down trees, cut them into four foot lengths but not stack them, at the rate of $1.00 to $1.50 per cord and 5 cents per stump for cedar poles. The latter job required cutting down the cedar tree and then limbing it. As the men were cutting the cordwood and the cedar, there would be two or three teams or yokes hauling out the cut wood and cedar on sleds to the landing. Out at the landing the wood would be unloaded onto the stack of the person who had done the cutting. At the end of the day the men were paid according to what was stacked in their piles. A cord a day was considered an average day's work. The goal was to get the wood out to a landing as fast as possible before a thaw turned the swamp into mud or a storm could bury the wood in snow. The wood cutters liked the Horton system because they did not have to stack wood in the swamp as was the usual custom and therefore could cut more and earn more than they could from most other contractors. Roy's father never had any trouble getting good wood cutters to work for him. Mr. Horton had a ready market for his wood. He used to furnish on contract wooden spiles (piles) for wharf and bridge work along the Taunton River, cedar poles for the oyster industry in Narragansett Bay, and stove wood. For years he had the contract to furnish firewood for the one room Dighton schools. He even contracted to supply ship timbers to the old ship yard at Fall River during World War I when wooden ships were still being built.

When Roy was about nine, his father began to let him drive by himself the empty sled and oxen from the landing back into the swamp to where Mr. Horton with his men and his sons were working. This was considered to be a boy's job because there was no load to manage and the oxen would go back on the path pretty much by themselves. After returning the sled to the loading site, Mr. Horton and his help would put on another load of wood and bind it in place with a chain, twisted in such a way with a twitch that the chain tightened up the load. If this twitch was not formed, by the time the logs reached the landing, they might have shifted against the chain so that it would not be possible to loosen the chain to get the load off. An iron load binder is used for the same purpose today.

For lighter hauling, like dragging out cedar poles, a special sled was made. It was similar to the logging sled but it was only about half as long. Several long pole butts were laid on the sled and tightened with a chain and twitch. Only the butts of the trees were supported on the sled while the small ends dragged on the ice. Often times a single horse was used for this work. Once the horse was started he would go along by himself to the landing. All Roy had to do was walk behind. Sometimes they had a horse so smart that it was only necessary to get him started and he would pull the load unattended to the landing. The person at the landing released the logs, turned the horse around, and sent him back again all by himself. That saved labor. "You couldn't do that with a tractor," said Roy.

As for farm tractors, they were useless for this type of work. In later years, about 1940, Roy's brother Raymond, who had taken over his father's farm, had bought a large International Tractor to do the farm work. When he tried driving it on the ice in the swamp, he found it could not even pull its own weight. Even though it had large diameter rear wheels, when one wheel got stuck behind a stump, the other wheel would just spin on the ice.

Roy recalled that all the cutting back then was done by two men with crosscut saws or with an ax. Once you could hear axes chopping away all over the swamp as woodsmen were getting their wood and timber out, unlike today when it is the whine of the chain saw that you hear. Roy remembered the last time he worked in the swamp: "I took along a chain saw. I didn't use it, but my son-in-law Francis McClellan who knows how to fell a tree did. He liked it, but I thought it was too fast. It was not hard to use, but you had to be alert. It does not stop because your knee gets in the way. The old crosscut saw had rhythm to it and you could relax more. The chain saw is constantly loud and hard on the ears. It is not like a man chopping with an axe. I like hearing the ringing of the axe."

Roy liked to talk about his boyhood experience in the swamps. He loved to cut wood in the winter. His father had taught him how to do it, just as Mr. Horton had learned from his father. Roy also loved to drive the oxen, and as he got older he enjoyed rolling the big logs onto the sled. It was especially fun at noon time in the swamp, Roy said. His mother had packed lunches, a fire was started, coffee was boiled, and everyone sat around the fire on logs eating and talking. Snow was on the ground, the wind would be blowing and it was cold, but Roy loved it.

Roy liked cutting white pine the best. In later years, after he got the pine out to the landing, Mr. Jillson, the owner of the sawmill where the Segregansett River crosses Williams Street in Dighton at the present Reed Farm, would come and load the logs on his truck for trips to the mill. He would saw them into anything Roy wanted, from boards to planking to two by fours. Roy said he liked the pine because he could use it in so many places and besides, it was nice to work with. Pine makes good corner posts, studs, and sheathing and when planed, it can be used for molding and finish work. Roy noted that he had built plenty of pine kitchen cabinets out of the native pine. Roy also found use for cedar, especially for shingles: native white cedar shingles were good although they often had a number of tight knots. They were no bother, however, if the shingles were painted. He had used plenty of them in his carpenter work. They also were thicker and weathered better than today's thin shingles. Once Roy shingled the barn roof for his father with these native shingles and they lasted for years.

In an interview with a reporter from the *Taunton Daily*

Gazette when he was 77 years old Roy was quoted: "Swamping was tough work. You could hardly drag your feet at night, but I always yearned to get into the swamp. When it would come winter, I would leave my men (carpenters' helpers) and go to the swamp to see if it had frozen thick enough. After I had worked two or three weeks at it, I was just about bushed out and I was ready to go back to carpentry which was easier work. It seemed as though you had to get it out of your blood. It was a challenge every year."

Roy also remembered at age 13 in 1912 helping his father draw cedar from the California Lot Swamp in Swansea and learning something new about handling a team of horses. The owner of the lot was Andrew Chace who lived on a farm a couple of miles away from the Horton farm at the corner of Sharp's Lot Road and Baker Road in Swansea. The California Lot was at the furthest rear corner of Mr. Chace's small but prosperous and efficient farm. Roy's father needed some cedar poles to fill out a contract with an oyster man. Mr. Horton was friendly with Andrew Chace and he knew Mr. Chace had a good stand of cedar in his swamp. After the business arrangements were made to buy the cedar, the Hortons' hired men appeared at the site and began cutting.

One day after the hired men had cut a sufficient quantity, Mr. Horton told Roy that he would be taking a yoke of oxen early that morning to the California Lot to begin hauling the cedar poles out to a landing on the edge of the swamp and that Roy was to come at noon with a team of horses and the large farm wagon to begin trucking the poles out over the cart path to Baker Road and on to the customer's pole yard. Roy recalled that he had no trouble harnessing the big work horses all by himself, hitching them to the wagon and arriving on time at the work site. After a noon time lunch at the landing, Mr. Horton and Roy loaded the wagon with a good size load of poles. Because the cart path they were to travel over was very rough with rocks and quite crooked, Mr. Horton hitched the yoke of oxen with a chain to the tongue of the wagon to assist the horses who could not have pulled the load alone over the rough path. As they started out toward the road, Mr. Horton stationed himself ahead, guiding the oxen while Roy sat up on the wagon driving the horses. At a sharp turn in the path Roy felt the wagon begin to lurch up and tip. Looking back, he saw the left rear wheel was riding up over the stone wall beside the path. Roy immediately yelled *"whoa"* and the whole rig came to a halt. Mr. Horton came back to the wagon and asked why he stopped the team. Roy pointed to the wagon wheel half up on top of the wall. Mr. Horton looked disgusted and said sternly: "Roy, don't you ever stop a team when they are pulling. It is better to let the wheel go over the wall and patch up any damage done later. But now to get going again we will have to take the wall apart, drive the wagon ahead, and then rebuild the wall; it's a lot more work." The lesson here that Roy said he never forgot was that once a team or a truck is stopped on an obstruction, it rarely can be started again until that obstacle is removed. This could be a rock or stump sticking up in the path. If the load is kept rolling, most times its momentum will roll it over the obstruction.

When the Hortons were working in Squannakonk Swamp, Roy said, they entered by Maple Lane. There was an old path that went into the south end of the Swamp from the end of Maple Lane, but usually they took a left at the end of the lane on to an ancient cart path leading north into the Swamp. Roy remembered that Ellery Goff of Rehoboth Village had set up a portable shingle mill in the early 1900's beside this path at the Bellanger Lot. Goff's men hauled the white cedar out to the mill, where it was sawn into shingles. The sawing machine was run by a steam engine fueled by wood scraps. There were paths all through the Swamp that had been used by woodsmen from the earliest settlement of Rehoboth. Roy noted that one such path went from the shingle mill path northerly across the Swamp to Vickery Point at the northeast corner of the Swamp and then on to the cart path and old road to the rear of his brother Elwood's farm on New Street. Elwood frequently cut wood in Squannakonk.

Squannakonk Swamp had a number of different landings besides those off Maple Lane. Sometimes the Hortons sledded wood to the landing south of Winthrop Street and hauled the wood home on the old cart path that went through present Breault Auto Sales property out to Winthrop Street, now blocked up. There was a landing near the Francis J. Wheeler farm on New Street that was often used by the Wheelers for charcoal burning. The cordwood was stacked here and later restacked into ricks for burning into charcoal. Further to the north on New Street there was another landing and a charcoal burning place on the property now owned by Vincent Cavallaro, also often used by the Wheelers. Hardly a trace of these sites remains today.

Roy once told me about a potentially dangerous experience he and his brother Elwood had had in Squannakonk Swamp. Elwood and Roy planned to cut pine at the Bellanger Lot off Maple Lane on February 14, 1940. Elwood came to the site from his farm with a sled and a yoke of oxen over the old path through the Swamp from Vickery Point. Roy met him there that morning after coming in from the Maple Lane path, having driven from his house on Wellington Street (formerly his grandfather's house) in a model A Ford. He drove in on the ancient path running off the lane as far as he could and turned around so the car pointed out. Roy recalled that it was a good thing he did. Soon after Elwood and Roy began cutting pine it began snowing. Although it started to snow quite hard, they kept working. Finally snow began to come down so thick they could only see a few feet in front of them and it was really piling up. The brothers finally decided that they had had enough for one day and Roy headed for his car while Elwood started home across the Swamp with the oxen and sled. The snow was so deep, Roy barely was able to drive out on the cart path onto Maple Lane. If he hadn't turned the car around so it was heading out, it would have stayed there until the snow melted in the spring. Meanwhile, Elwood got started for home with the oxen and sled on the path to Vickery Point, but the snow was coming down so thick he could hardly see a thing. He completely lost his bearings and could not distinguish the path from the rest of the Swamp through the swirling snow. However, the oxen plodded steadily along, and since they seemed to know where they were going, Elwood unhitched the sled, let them go, and followed behind. Sure enough, after what seemed an endless walk, his barn yard appeared up out of the gloom. Elwood always said that if he hadn't had those oxen with him, he would have been in a serious situation and might never had made it home. This snow storm was the record setting blizzard of 1940 that became known as the St. Valentine's Day Blizzard. In its wake it left about 24 inches of snow on the level and drifts many times that height. It was unmatched in the last two centuries except perhaps by the Blizzard of 1888 and the biggest one of them all, the Great Blizzard of February, 1978.

Roy told me of other swamp experiences he had as an adult. After he had established his own business, he spent more time in Manwhague Swamp than in the other swamps. He would enter on the old Stony Path at the Sign Board, the corner of Cedar and Gorham Street, and cross the Holden land to the north edge of the Swamp. Near that edge flowed the Rocky Run, a good sized brook that had to be crossed and was a little bit of an obstacle. There was an old bridge there that usually had to be repaired. Roy had been all through that Swamp and knew every bit of it. In 1927, he bought the timber on the Moulton Lot on the north end of the Swamp from the Horton family. His father did own some Moulton land but not this lot, which was owned by the heirs of Samuel Horton (no relation) whose dairy farm was on the westerly border of the Swamp on Plain Street. The Horton farm was named "Manwhague" after the Swamp. Roy made arrangements to buy the pines from that lot through Samuel's widow, Jennie Horton. Roy recalled that he cut some nice pines there. He landed the logs near where the old Lindley Horton House once stood, loaded them on Mr. Jillson's big hard rubber tired logging truck, and hauled them out over the Lindley Path to near the corner of Plain and Brook Streets and on to his sawmill on Williams Street, Dighton.

Roy was interviewed once about an experience in Manwhague Swamp he had cutting a white pine: "This pine grew in amongst the cedars and it went way up. It did not grow thick like some grow, but it was tall. I did not know how I was going to fell it. You have to look to see which way that pine wants to fall. You look at the pine and see which way the heavy limbs have grown and which way she might lean. Then you have to take into consideration the wind direction. That is very important because wind can take a pine over with her heavy top. If you fell it with the wind, you will have no problem, but sometimes you cannot do this as many large maples are in the way. You have to get it in between these trees. It is quite a little trick. Well, I got five 12 foot lengths which is 60 feet from that large pine. The top where the last cut was made was a foot through. That was the biggest one, not the biggest around, but the one that went up the furthest; the first and second cuts were about the same size. Generally they taper and you can notice it, but that pine was a dandy tree."

Henry Wheaton Horton hauling a load of wood home on Reservoir Avenue Rehoboth, circa 1939, from the landing at the foot of Long Hill.

The idea of a logging railroad being built into Manwhague Swamp has always intrigued me. So little is known about the railroad, there is some questions whether or not if it really existed; it could almost be called "The Mystery Swamp Railroad." The proposal of the Joseph Lunan Company to build this railroad to facilitate the hauling out the cedar and pine timber always seemed to be a unique and interesting method of overcoming the hazards encountered by sudden thaws when using draft animals and sleds. Over the years I have heard rumors of such a railroad from various sources, but no one could ever give any details about where it was located and how it was powered, by horse or engine, or even if it did once exist at all. Roy told me he had heard of it but he never knew anything about it nor had ever seen any remnants or ruins from it during his numerous travels through that swamp. The Reverend George H. Tilton, writing about the Lunan logging operation in 1917 in his History of Rehoboth, said: "In 1910-13 Joseph Lunan and Sons of Fall River operated their mill on the border of this swamp and built a corduroy road into its midst, cutting off not only the vast cedar supply, but also the magnificent pine timber..." He however made no mention of the railroad in his account. To my knowledge the only person living today who knows a few of the details of that logging operation is Ernest Moe Horton, Jr. who has lived all his life on the Horton farm "Manwhague", as did his father. Moe told me that his father said the railroad was a light rail affair, powered by a small gasoline driven engine. The railroad began on the lane leading westerly from the sharp bend in Hornbine Road at the present Everett Gonsalves property and ran westerly into the swamp almost to the other side near the Lindley Place on the north shore. Moe said his father often visited the logging and railroad area to be sure the Lunan Company was not cutting on to the Horton Swamp lots. Also, Moe was told by his father that the Lunan Company had set up their steam driven sawmill on the Gonsalves Lane and later moved it to a new site at Log Neck on the west shore of the swamp in the rear of the present Rehoboth Sanitary Land Fill. This took place after their logging operation was moved to the lower end of the swamp. Moe, too, like Roy never saw any signs of this activity. "It was way before my time," Moe said.

SQUANNAKONK SWAMP, REHOBOTH

by Betsey Dexter Dyer

Composed after a visit to the swamp in the winter of 1973 by Betsey and Otis Dyer.

Low wetland of cedar and springs
Roots in ice and roots in water
Woodlot clearing where axes ring
Pasture lands define the border.

Spring melts and floods the muddy ground
Now grow skunk cabbage and ferns
The woods are green and full of sound
Of peepers and birds returned.

Moist heat of summer, no breeze
Mosquitoes hot in the swarming air
Almost dry, the dead fern leaves
Slow streams trickle here and there.

Autumn days are red and cool
Crisp leaves on chilly ground
Frosty patterns on the standing pool
Are frozen when the sun goes down.

The first freeze of the year
The wind is still, the air is dry
Light snow is tracked by rabbit and deer
Branches stand white against the sky.

A lone hunter stalking rabbit and fox
hears the startled bluejay call
Then steady blows of a distant ax
Then shouted orders as trees fall.

Wood smooth against the calloused palms
Blade flashes through the air
Graceful and steady, the woodsman's arms
Each blow is strong and fair.

A few minutes long, the pine withstood
Then balance cut and weakened by the blows
The tree cleared a path through brittle wood
Fell deeply into the crusted snow.

Where men with blades must saw
And spray the yellow sawdust
And then the teams of oxen draw
The sleds breaking through the crust.

After an ice storm in the night
The hunter walks through fairyland
All is glittering, crystal and white
The dawn shines through with rainbow bands.

Here beads of ice on the bent twig bark
Gleam like slow motion photography
On water droplets flung in an arc
From branch tips of rain tossed tree.

Through the swamp, a tinkling sound
Of shifting ice. As axes fall
Diamonds shower brightly to the ground
And then the sun melts all.

Each cold day the wood is loaded and hauled
To steam powered saws on the landings
That during winter months were there installed
And to the charcoal pits, constantly smouldering.

Once Elwood Horton, driving his yoke home
Was caught in a blizzard and lost the way
So he loosened the yoke and let the oxen roam
They headed right to the barnyard and their hay.

A thick old maple bent like a bow
What wind could make it bow its head?
A tiny sapling tied down years ago
By Roy Horton waiting for his father's sled.

First thaw and the woods are still
No axes, teams, and woodsmen
Charcoal still smokes a little on hill
but the flames will not be fired up again.

The hunter sees the swamp become spring
The solid land, where in winter he strode
Melts into streams and wet green openings
And water seeps over swampy woodlot roads.

Chapter III

WOODLOTS

Roy's father owned a number of woodlots in the eastern part of Rehoboth and West Dighton. Although as a young man he had bought from his own father or purchased from his brother Gaius a considerable amount of land, he was always in need of more woodlots to supply his thriving firewood and timber business. Many of these woodlots were purchased not for their white cedar and pine but for the hardwood needed for the Horton stove wood business. Because of this extensive wood business, Roy's father in 1907 had a telephone put in, the very first installed in the Wellington Street section of Dighton. The line was strung in from Rehoboth where a telephone office had recently been installed. Since the Hortons' phone was included in the original Rehoboth telephone exchange, when phones of additional subscribers were added, their phones were connected to the same exchange. Because of this practice phones in West Dighton are still serviced by the Rehoboth exchange to this day. Very few people had phones then because they were expensive. "Everyone would come to our house to use ours," Roy recalled.

Some of the Hortons' woodlots were purchased at land auctions held about 1900 when the estate of two brothers, George N. Moulton (1821-1895) and John B. Moulton (1821-1891), were dispersed. The Moulton brothers were twins and were descended from an old Rehoboth family that lived for several generations on a farm on Moulton Street, Rehoboth. Besides inheriting their home farm and many other outlying lots and other farms from their father, they had also purchased together over the years a considerable number of additional woodlots, all in Rehoboth. The brothers were bachelors, lived together during their final years at the corner of Brook and Pleasant Streets, and were considered eccentric. They were called "land poor" because all their money was tied up in their farms and woodlots. Since their estates were complicated by their common land ownership, the Probate Court in order to unravel their joint assets held a series of land auctions and sold their woodlots off to the highest bidder. Henry Horton attended these land auctions and bought several parcels in the easterly part of Rehoboth that were situated close enough to his home so he could reach them with a fairly short journey. One of these lots on the east side of Simmons Street was known as the 6 Rod Way Lot. This is the lot that has the old Elder Enoch Goff baptism pool on it. Roy remembered his father cutting wood there beginning in the winter of 1910. Other Moulton lots purchased in the area were the Long Hill Lots at the foot of Long Hill on the north side of Reservoir Avenue near Simmons Street. The Hortons began cutting here in 1915 when Roy was in high school, and they also worked here during the winters of 1917 and 1918. These lots were on the border of Bad Luck Swamp where the Hortons owned many other swamp lots.

The Hortons used the old landing on the Moulton land on the northwesterly side of Reservoir Avenue near Simmons Street to land the cordwood cut from both the Moulton Lots, Sprague Lot, and the other Bad Luck Lots. Here Mr. Horton set up a cordwood sawing machine driven by a one cylinder gasoline engine to cut the 4 foot lengths of wood into stove wood. Roy recalled spending many Saturdays at the landing during the fall helping his father cut up the logs into stove lengths. When the four foot logs were cut in half, there were two 24 inch pieces; when cut in thirds, there were three 16 inch pieces; and when cut into quarters, there were four 12 inch pieces, which were all standard stove lengths. Roy recalled that not only did the 48 inch lot divide up nicely but it also was the best size to handle in the woods and the most stable when carried on a sled. Usually it was not necessary to split the cordwood before sawing, as is often the case today, because the woodlands had been cut off so often that the trees had no time to grow to the sizes we now see.

Another woodlot purchase, very important to the Hortons, was the David W. Francis land lying between New Street in Rehoboth and Horton Street in Dighton. This land consisted of the many lots that Mr. Francis had bought from various people over the years during the latter part of the nineteenth century. In the early 1800's this land was part of Elder Enoch Goff's farm and comprised much of the land I was surveying for the Dighton-Rehoboth School District in 1959 when I first met Roy. Some of these lots at the time of the Francis purchase were still being cultivated, but the majority of them had reverted back to woodland. Connected with this property was the old Elder Enoch Goff house, which in the mid 1800's was occupied by Shubael Goff. By the time Mr. Horton purchased these lots, Shubael had been dead for years; yet his name had sort of stuck to the area. His first name being Shubael, the Hortons often referred to the place as "over at Shube's" or "over at Shubael's."

Mr. Francis lived on New Street in Rehoboth where he died in 1913, leaving a widow, a daughter Mary, and a son David, Jr. called Darby. Mr. Horton was interested in buying these lots after Francis had died, but it was not until a few years later in 1919 that he heard that the Francis heirs were interested in selling. At that time Mrs. Francis and her daughter were living in East Longmeadow, Massachusetts, and Darby was dead. Roy was attending Taunton High School when his father asked him to go over to the Registry of Deeds in Taunton after school to copy off the Francis deeds. After studying the deeds, Roy found it fun to walk over the land with his father, trying to decide what the land could best be used for. Mr. Horton was enthusiastic about owning these lots and soon arranged the sale with the widow, all through the mail. The Hortons used some of the land for growing strawberries, corn, and hay, and from the woodland, they cut cords of wood for the Horton wood business.

By 1959 the cultivated land had been abandoned for some time and so grown up into brush and briers that I could hardly recognize its former use. Over the later years some of the lots had also acquired quite a growth of heavy pine. In 1960 just before construction began on the Regional School, Roy tried to make arrangements with the School Building Committee to cut the pine for lumber on the Francis land that Roy had sold to the Regional School District. He was referred by the Committee to the architects in Providence who told him that nothing could be cut because as many trees as possible were to be preserved for landscaping around the school. Roy said that when

"Over at Shube's" today, the present Dighton-Rehoboth Regional School.

the contractor arrived to begin construction no attempt at preservation was made. It made his heart sick to see the big bulldozers shove all that nice firewood and timber up into piles and burn it. He was glad his father did not have to see it. Of course by then, fuel oil was so cheap you could not give firewood away, he added, and few people knew the value of native white pine lumber, particularly Providence architects and contractors.

There were a number of local people available whom the Hortons could hire to cut wood. Some did it on a part-time basis when work was slow at their major place of employment. Roy noted that all tradespeople, including himself, had slow times, usually during the winter when they looked for other employment. For others cutting was their year round occupation. These latter woodsmen, to be close to the job, sometimes erected small cabins deep in the woods to live in while working on a woodlot large enough to warrant this extra work. The sites of these cabins can be identified today by the remains of stone heaps that once supported the cabin sills, a rusty cot the wood cutter used for a bed, and some old kitchen blue coated metal utensils rusting away under the leaves. After Henry W. Horton had retired from the wood business, his son Raymond carried it on well into the 1940's, mostly selling fireplace wood. Since it was becoming difficult to find wood cutters willing to build or live in these crude shacks in the woods, at Raymond's request Roy designed and built a small cabin mounted on a farm type trailer or cart. Inside there were a small table and stove and a pair of bunks for a couple of workers. A farm tractor was used to move this rig from woodlot to woodlot. This cabin was used by Raymond's choppers until the early 1940's when it was burned by vandals while parked on Wellington Street.

Chapter IV

ELDER ENOCH GOFF, YANKEE PREACHER

Because of his strong character and influence in the West Dighton - East Rehoboth neighborhood, further reference should be made to Elder Enoch Goff (1740-1810), the founder of what is now known as the West Dighton Christian Congregational Church. I met his name often in 1959 while surveying at the proposed Dighton-Rehoboth Regional High School site. Even though Elder Goff had been dead for 170 years, I was surprised to meet so many people living today who had heard of him in some way in connection with either the Church or the neighborhood. Many people living in Rehoboth and Dighton are descendants of Elder Goff, including Roy Horton and his family. For over two hundred years Elder Goff's Church and later the West Dighton Christian Church played an important part in the lives of the Horton family; Roy, his father Henry W. Horton, and his grandfather James H. Horton all had served as Trustees of the Church. Originally founded by Elder Goff as a Baptist Church, it was converted to the Congregational denomination in 1930.

Roy once pointed out to me, just as his father had once shown him, the spot where the church originally stood at the southwesterly corner of Cedar Street and Purchase Street in Rehoboth, just over the Dighton line. That church was built in 1780, a rustic structure furnished with rough wooden benches. It no longer exists. This building, however, was not Elder Goff's first church. Old records state that a group of Rehoboth and Dighton citizens in 1771, feeling the need to establish a Baptist Church near to their neighborhood, began holding services in a barn.

Supposedly it was in this barn that Elder Goff was ordained as a Baptist minister or Elder. The congregation prospered, so

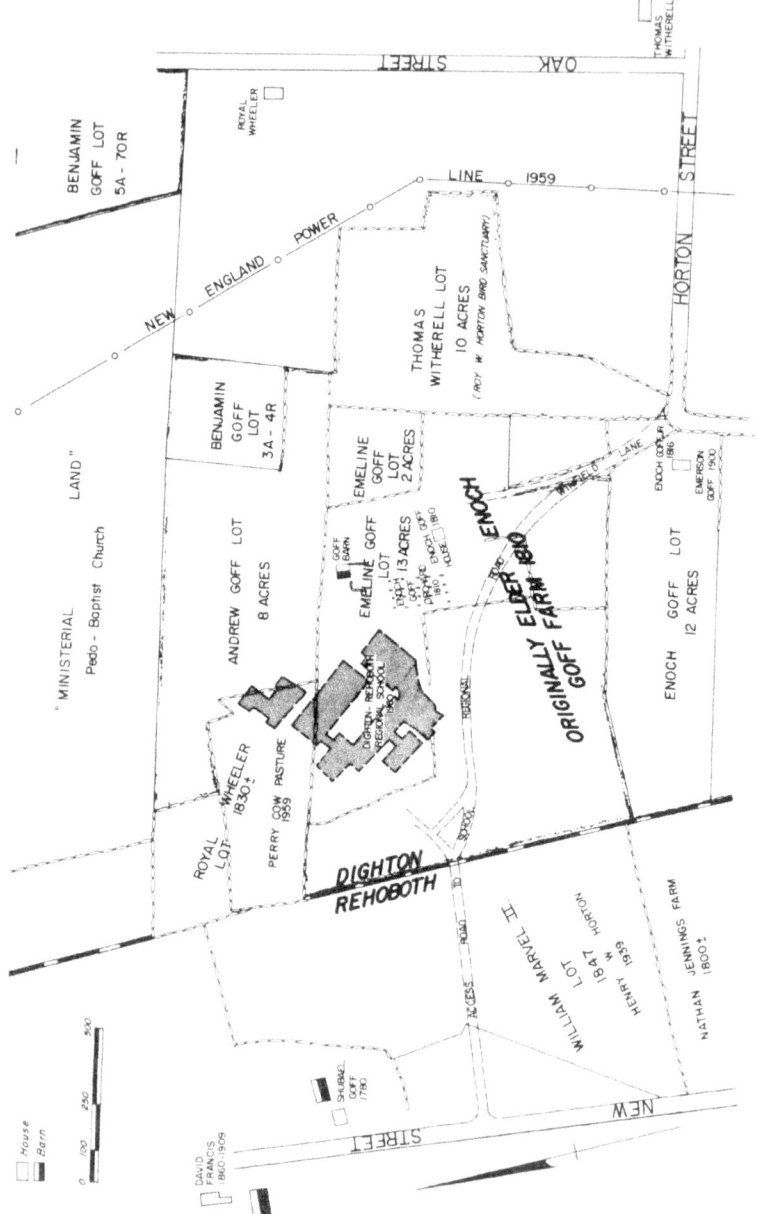

THE FORMER ELDER ENOCH GOFF FARM AND THE LOTS "OVER AT SHUBE'S" PURCHASED BY THE HORTON'S FROM DAVID W. FRANCIS IN 1919
Now the site of the Dighton-Rehoboth Regional High School

Elder Goff's Meeting House, built 1796, the present West Dighton Christian Congregational Church at the corner of Horton Street and Wellington Street on Goff Hill, West Dighton.

that in 1796 the present church could be built on the corner of Horton Street and Wellington Street in West Dighton on top of the hill, subsequently known as Goff's Hill, for a cost of $1,934.52. An old account described Elder Goff as follows: "Until his death in 1810, Elder Goff was the pastor. He was uneducated but had a great force of character and personal magnetism. He gathered a force of over three hundred in a sparsely settled area. Invited to preside over a large church in Providence, he answered he could not leave his family parishioners; and in truth his family looked to him for advice of all kinds. He had no salary but supported himself by making shoes."

The account should have also mentioned that shoemaking was not his only source of support, because Elder Goff also owned and operated a 96 acre farm at the present site of the Dighton-Rehoboth Regional High School which ran from Winfield Lane and Horton Street on the east in Dighton to New Street on the West in Rehoboth. There is presently a house at the end of Winfield Lane that is situated on the same foundation as the original Goff home, having replaced the original after it burned down many years ago, before Roy was born. Once, when Roy was telling me about Elder Goff and his farm he squinted his eyes, gazed off in the distance and said, "I can see the old Goff house now, a little gambrel half house up the lane, a tiny little thing, like they used to build." Roy's father had seen the old house before it burned, had described it to Roy, and Roy was imagining what it looked like from his father's recollection. The only structure that still stands on the old Goff farm is the house that was built in the late eighteenth century for Elder Goff's son Shubael, and is now owned by Angela Bilodeau at 165 New Street in Rehoboth.

The Hortons always had a close association with the Goff farm. After Elder Goff's death, the farm was divided among his numerous children with each heir receiving a large "set off" of land. It was some of these lots that were eventually acquired

The only original building left on the Enoch Goff Farm is at 165 New Street, Rehoboth. The house was built for his son Shubael, circa 1780. It is now the house of Angela Bilodeau.

by David W. Francis and later purchased by Henry W. Horton from the Francis heirs in 1919. After the Francis purchase, one time or another, most of the Horton family spent some time "over at Shube's" as they sometimes called this Goff farm. When Raymond, Roy's brother, was married in 1917, Raymond and his new wife moved into the Horton homestead on Wellington Street. Since Henry W. Horton and his wife soon found that the old farm house had become too crowded, shortly after the purchase from Mr. Francis they moved in "over at Shube's." Later when Roy and Elsie were married, this farm became their first home. The Hortons used the old Goff fields to raise crops and the woodland for firewood. Roy's brother, Raymond, also made use of the old place by using the large sheds located on the property to store fertilizer when he was the agent for the Miller Fertilizer Company. Raymond sold fertilizer to many of the Dighton truck garden farmers.

About 20 years ago Roy asked me if I would like to see the place where Elder Goff used to baptize his parishioners. According to Roy, the baptism pool was located deep in the woods off the corner of Cedar and Simmons Streets. It was used as such in the latter part of the eighteenth century while the church was located in Rehoboth at the corner of Cedar and Purchase Streets. When Roy was twelve years old in 1911 his father had taken him there and he wanted to do the same for me. I did want to see it, but because we never could find a mutually convenient time, that day never came. It was not until 1991, two years after Roy's death, that I finally had the opportunity to view the pool. I approached it by walking in easterly from Simmons Street in Rehoboth, though Roy said he and his father had walked in to the site on an old cart path leading in by the present Duffy house on Reservoir Avenue in Rehoboth. The whole area today is covered with a heavy growth of hard wood. The pool was just as Roy described it to me. It was dug out of a fairly low area, but not swampy, to a depth of about four feet in the center. Along its long axis the pool was about 20 feet long and stoned up on both sides. The shorter ends were about eight feet wide, had no walls, and were dug so that the pool bottom sloped gradually down from both ends to the four foot depth at the center. This allowed easy access and exit to and from the pool for the people when baptisms were taking place. A line could be kept moving through the pool.

By the mid nineteenth century, the use of the pool for baptism had long been forgotten and the owner was calling it a watering place for his cattle; a subsequent owner thought the stoned up walls were bridge abutments. It is easy to see why

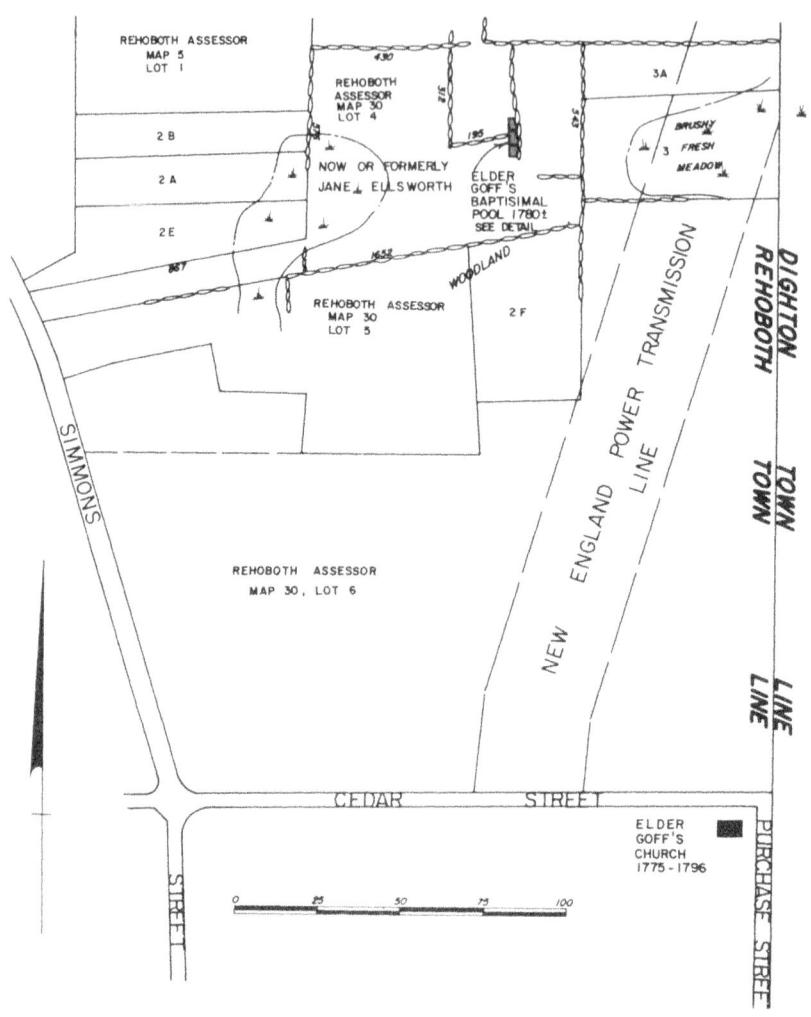

LOCATION OF ELDER ENOCH GOFF'S FIRST CHURCH AND
BAPTISMAL POOL
Rehoboth, circa 1780

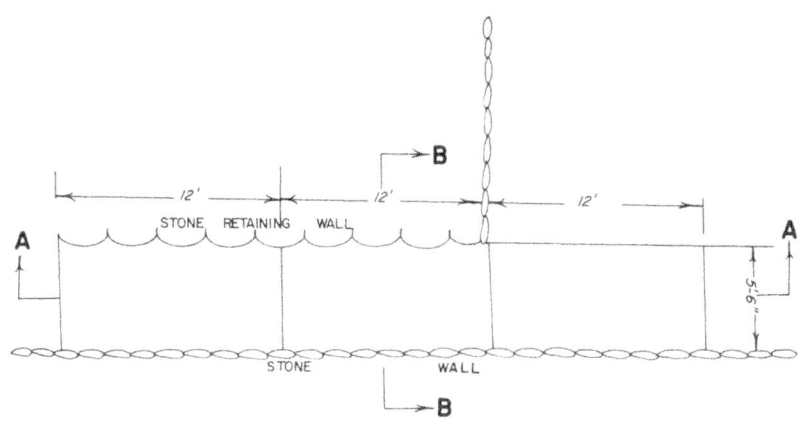

PLAN VIEW

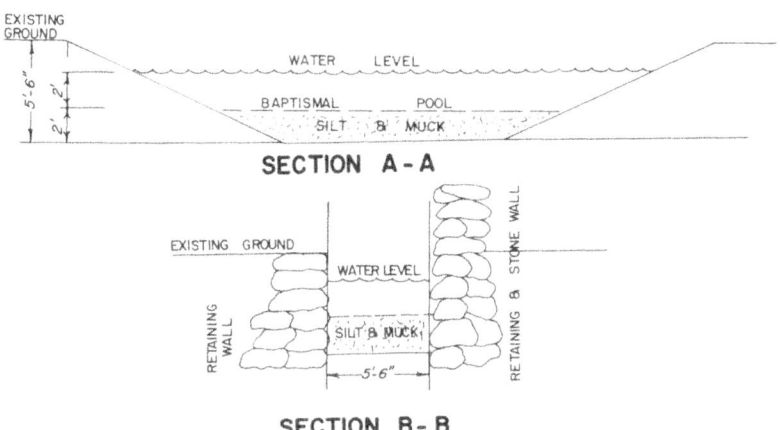

SECTION A-A

SECTION B-B

DETAIL PLAN OF ELDER GOFF'S BAPTISMAL POOL
Rehoboth, circa 1780

E. Otis Dyer, Jr. at the old Enoch Goff baptismal pool, circa 1790 off Simmons Street, Rehoboth.

someone might think it had been built for a place for cattle to drink, but it is surprising that anyone would connect it with a bridge structure because there is no stream. The only reason we know its true use today is the result of historical information passed down through generations in the Horton family; Roy learned about it from his father who in turn was told about it by his father, James H. Horton. James' father, Benson Horton, probably heard about it from his grandfather, Barnet Horton. Since Barnet had a farm nearby at the time when the pool was still being actively used, he would have been aware of its true use. After studying the site, I came to the conclusion that it may have been originally built for a pool to wash sheep and later also found to be a convenient place to hold baptisms. The easy entrance and exit ramps would have made it easy to drive a flock of sheep through for washing before shearing.

Once when Roy and I were standing in front of the old Goff Church admiring the late eighteenth century architecture, Roy said that when he was a boy it was discovered that some of the big supporting timbers in the belfry had become dangerously rotten from rain driving in the open windows. Mr. Briggs of Dighton, an excellent carpenter of the old school, and his men were hired to replace the defective timbers. Because even then

Roy was interested in carpentry and anything to do with wood, it was fascinating for him to watch Mr. Briggs and his men cut out the rotten pieces and frame in new timber. Not only was this heavy work, but it had to be done at a dizzying height. There were no truck cranes available to lift the heavy loads as there are today; everything had to be rigged into place with ropes from high scaffolds. Roy said he has warned the young men of the church more than once to keep an eye on that belfry, not to let the rain get in there and rot the wood again.

After Roy died in January 1989 in his 90th year, a beautiful memorial service was held in Elder Goff's Church. The Church was packed from floor to gallery with people who came to honor Roy.*

---

* See Appendix I, page 183 for the eulogy given by Frank Coughlan in memory of Roy at the Memorial service.

GENEALOGICAL CHART OF ROY W. HORTON'S DESCENT FROM ELDER ENOCH GOFF

(1) Elder Enoch Goff   m.   Deborah Talbot
     b. 1740   b. 1740
     d. 1810   d. 1816

(2) Benjamin Goff   m.   Eleanor Beers (2nd husband: Job Wheeler)
     b. 1782   b. 1787
     d. 1832   d. 1871

(3) Eleanor Goff   m.   James W. Paul
     b. 1815   b. 1814
     d. 1867   d. 1873

(4) Mary Asneth Paul   m.   James Harlan Horton
     b. 1843   b. 1837
     d. 1915   d. 1907

(5) Henry Wheaton Horton   m.   Hannah J. Leonard
     b. 1864   b. 1866
     d. 1943   d. 1942

(6) Roy Wheaton Horton
     b. 1899
     d. 1989

The David W. Francis House at 156 New Street, Rehoboth. Note the architectural style is similar to that of George Hathaway Goff House at 66 New Street on page 136.

Chapter V

WOOD OPERATORS

The people that interested Roy and his family the most were the wood operators, as Roy liked to call them. The three wood operators Roy talked about most lived along the west side of New Street in Rehoboth. Their farms straddled that road and ran deep in the rear into the woodlands of Squannakonk Swamp. Apparently there were no wood operators living in West Dighton, except the Hortons, or at least Roy never mentioned any. To be really successful in the wood business, it was first necessary to have a prosperous dairy farm. The two, woodcutting and dairying, seemed to go hand in hand. Perhaps the West Dighton farms were less fertile or the farmers there lacked the initiative to emulate the success of their neighbors on New Street. Roy recalled that the three things the wood operators seemed to have in common were that each had a prosperous dairy farm of about 15 to 30 milking cows, each sold firewood and timber, and each achieved the height of his business career in the latter decades of the nineteenth century, a period when firewood in neighboring cities was in a very high demand for fuel. Much of the equipment used in dairying, such as wagons, sleds, and horse teams, was the same as used in the wood business. The hired men needed to work on the dairy farm could be employed during the winter in the woods and swamps to cut the next year's firewood supply and to haul it out to the landings and storage yards after the summer and fall farm work of planting, cultivating, haying, and harvesting had been completed. Perhaps other advantages the New Street farmers may have had over any competitors living in West Dighton were their easy access to the vast woodlands in Squannakonk Swamp at the rear of their farms and their proximity to the Providence and Pawtucket markets.

Living at the Winthrop Street end of New Street, the first operator mentioned by Roy was George Hathaway Goff. Besides being very active in the wood, dairy, and vegetable business, Goff also made and sold charcoal. The next farm to the south was the home of Francis J. Wheeler and his father Jasper. They also both farmed and conducted a large wood and charcoal business. Next to the Wheelers' farm was a farm owned by David W. Francis, a successful but somewhat controversial wood dealer and farmer, a man the Hortons were somewhat in awe of.

There were also a number of other men engaged in the dairy and wood business who might be called minor wood operators. This category would have included Henry Wheaton Horton; Arthur H. Goff, the son of George H. Goff, who took over his father's farm after his father's death in 1903; Lester A. Waterman, whose farm was at the corner of New Street and County Street; and Samuel E. Smith who conducted a farming and wood business about a mile to the north of the corner of New Street and Winthrop Street on Francis Street. The only thing that set these people apart from the big operators was that although they were very hard working and enterprising, their success was limited by the declining demand of the use of the wood as fuel during the period they were in business in the first decades of this century. The bottom fell out of the firewood market after World War I when kerosene space heaters began to be manufactured in quantity and the price of kerosene went to five cents per gallon. Wood stoves could not compete with the low fuel prices nor provide the steady heat as the new heater did 24 hours a day. The farmers still in the wood business gradually dropped the selling of stove wood and began to supply the growing fireplace wood market, a never very profitable enterprise. According to Roy, sometime in the latter part of the nineteenth century and once during World War I there were fuel shortages; Roy was told by his father that many people in the cities of Providence and Pawtucket, who heated their houses with coal or wood, would be so desperate for firewood during one of these shortages that the wood operators in Rehoboth would sell out at high prices and "clean up."

DAVID W. FRANCIS

The wood operator who impressed the Hortons most was David W. Francis (1841-1913) who lived at 156 New Street, Rehoboth. The Hortons did not always approve of his business methods, but they were very impressed with his ability to make money. Like the other wood operators, Mr. Francis had a prosperous dairy farm, but his main business was selling firewood, spiles, and cedar poles. In later years, using some of his profits from that business, he became a sort of small private local banker, loaning money out to people in the form of personal loans and mortgages. Roy remembered seeing Mr. Francis as an old man sitting in the front window of his house on New Street when Roy used to go up to Wheeler's Corner to catch the trolley for High School in Taunton. Roy never saw Mr. Francis do any work himself during these later years of his life. He always had several hired men on the farm to look after things. Besides the hired men, Mr. Francis always had a few characters hanging around the farm trying to pick up a few dollars by doing odd jobs. He had a reputation for being a hard man to work for and a skinflint. Francis had made the bulk of his money by cutting cordwood on his numerous wood and swamp lots and hauling it in his wagons for sale in Pawtucket, Rhode Island.

When a fuel shortage occurred, perhaps because of a railroad or coal mine strike, Mr. Francis was always ready to take advantage of it. Roy was told by his father that during a shortage Mr. Francis would line up six or seven farm wagons, one behind the other, and load them up with four foot lengths of cordwood. Each wagon load, pulled by one horse, was driven to the coal and wood yard in Pawtucket for sale. To save on labor, each horse was tied to the wagon ahead so only one driver was needed. Some horses had been so well trained for this work that they could be trusted to hold their position in the wagon train without even being tied. The lone driver, sitting on the lead wagon and running the whole procession, was usually the Hortons' neighbor, Emerson Goff, one of Mr. Francis' trusted hired men.

If Mr. Goff and his string of wagons arrived on the streets of Pawtucket during a fuel shortage, sometimes his wagons would be emptied before he reached the wood dealer's yard.

People would be so desperate for the wood they would stop the wagon train in the street, bargain for, and buy the wood right there. With the price adjusted according to this demand, David Francis would "clean up." The big barn on his farm was full of horses kept for this purpose. Several yoke of oxen were also kept for the heavy hauling in the woods. Later as the demand for wood began to decline, Mr. Francis cut back and enlarged his dairy somewhat.

Much of Mr. Francis' profits from his wood business had been shrewdly re-invested into mortgages and loans to his neighbors. There was one small farm on New Street, not far from his own home, which he sold and held the mortgage for. When the purchaser got behind on the mortgage payments, Mr. Francis was quick to foreclose, take the property back, and repeat the procedure with another buyer. This procedure went on several times with several different owners. Roy said that Mr. Francis made about as much money on selling and foreclosing that little farm as on anything he did. When he died in 1913, Francis held 30 promissory notes and mortgages against various people, totalling over $14,000.00, a large sum for those times.

The prosperity of the Francis family showed in the new home they built for themselves. Most houses of that period had simple lines, but the Francis house had bay windows and other architectural embellishments and ornamentations not generally seen in the area. The house had a front porch and two large bay windows; cornices and eaves were prominent and the workmanship was excellent. Roy, who as a carpenter had worked on almost all the houses in the area, added that the next house up the street built for George H. Goff at 66 New Street now owned by Abner Hall, was apparently built by the same carpenter who had built the Francis house. These house styles are known as "Carpenter Gothic," a style of architectural decoration that mimicked traditional European stone work Gothic. This could be done in wood by ordinary carpenters once power driven saws and molding machines were perfected. The Francis house had been built over the ruins of an earlier and simpler house that dated from before the Revolution. In the cellar, evidence of old charred timbers indicates the original house may have burned down. David Francis, shortly after he returned to Rehoboth from service in the Civil War, had purchased the farm from his father, Bradford Francis.

Roy told me a story about his father and David Francis. Roy's father was about 14 years old in 1870 when he used to earn a few dollars working for Mr. Francis by using his father's horses to haul cordwood out of the swamp. Mr. Francis, then about thirty years old, worked with his team right along with Roy's father. After a load of wood was drawn out to the road and unloaded, Mr. Francis, not allowing his team to rest, would trot his horses quickly back into the woods for another load. He wanted Mr. Horton to do the same with his team, but Roy's father, although only a boy, had sense enough not to do it because it was very hard on the horses. Mr. Francis didn't care about that. He was always trying to get the most out of everything.

Roy added that Mr. Francis had two sons by two wives: David W., Jr. (1890-1918) called "Darby" and Frederick E. (1873-1906). Roy did not think Darby was too bright. He was Fred's half brother and nothing like him. Darby either enlisted or was drafted into the army during World War I and died in the Army, not from combat, but from pneumonia in Syracuse, New York, during the virulent influenza epidemic of the winter of 1918-1919. Roy's brother Raymond also lost his first wife to that sickness. Roy heard that Fred was a lot like his father and was favored by him. He was born of the earlier marriage, never married, and lived on the farm with his family. He was also an operator in the wood business. Roy did not remember him because he died when Roy was only six. Mr. Horton said Fred died in great pain with colic or acute indigestion, but according to Roy it may have been a ruptured appendix — probably the doctors knew nothing about it. Fred died at the Francis home at age 33 on January 14, 1906, with the family doctor and lawyer at his bedside. When it was seen that Fred had not long to live, the lawyer was called in to prepare the will which left all his property to his father. Fred, like his father, was a shrewd businessman and had accumulated considerable property for a young man, mostly in the form of woodlots. A newspaper article written at the time said that "Mr. Francis was a young man highly esteemed by all who knew him."

Although David Francis had considerable wealth and was

one of the richest men then living in Rehoboth, he did not have a happy family life. His first wife Elizabeth A. M. Wheeler, the mother of Fred, had died young in 1880 at age 28, also supposedly of appendicitis. Two years later, David married Mary A. Chace of Somerset, Massachusetts, a woman fifteen years younger than himself. David and his new wife had two children. At the time of Fred's death these two children were thirteen and fifteen years old, respectively. For some time the father had not been getting along with his new family and his marriage to Mary had ended in divorce, an almost unheard thing at that time. Perhaps part of their marital problems was caused by their son Darby's strange behavior. The general consensus of people who knew Darby was that his personality was the opposite of that of his father and half-brother which made family differences inevitable. These family problems were perhaps the reason David had called in the lawyer on the day Fred died, to draw up Fred's will to be sure that no one in his second family shared in his son's estate.

However, if it was David's intention to prevent his divorced wife and children from inheriting his son's property and his own estate, it did not work out that way. Seven years later, on December 9, 1913, when David died, his divorced wife and daughter Mary were living in Saugus. Since neither the mother or father had wanted anything to do with him, Darby was living with his Aunt Ella Chace, a sister of David's divorced wife, in an apartment on the Francis J. Wheeler farm, the next farm up New Street from the Francis' home. Because David died unexpectedly from a stroke and had failed to make out a will, his entire estate passed to his children Mary and Darby. Since Mary was a minor, David's divorced wife was appointed her guardian. Just what David had tried to prevent seven years earlier happened; his second family acquired complete control of his property. Mary and her two children began immediately to liquidate his large land holdings. The first to go within a year of his death was his 90 acre homestead farm on both sides of New Street. Soon after, they began disposing of the many woodlots David had owned, one of them as large as 45 acres. This was the situation when the Hortons in 1919 purchased from Mary and her two children the Francis lots in the vicinity of what is now the Dighton-Rehoboth Regional High School, "over at Shubael's".

Darby, living with his Aunt Ella on the Wheeler homestead on New Street, came into a considerable inheritance as his father's property was sold off. He had fun spending it and no longer had to work, if he ever did. One of the first things he bought was a new Overland car. Next he had a garage built on the Wheeler farm to house it in, probably one of the first garages to be built in Rehoboth. Aunt Ella, of course, knowing Darby had inherited money, tried to get him to pay a portion of the rent and board. Since Darby did not like to be nagged about that, just to spite his aunt, he would take a handful of bills from his wallet and burn them up in front of her.

While engaged in his favorite pastime of driving his new Overland car, Darby showed he had a kind streak by often inviting the neighborhood children to ride in his car, sometimes taking them on excursions to the beach at Plymouth and on Cape Cod. There were probably few children in Rehoboth at that time before World War I who ever had an opportunity to ride in a car, let alone go to visit the seashore in one.

Little can be seen today in Dighton and Rehoboth of the extensive farm and business enterprises which David W. Francis and his son Fred worked so hard to establish. Their ornate Carpenter Gothic style house still stands at 156 New Street. Beside the house their large New England style barn that once housed the numerous work horses, dairy cows, and cattle was neglected and was blown down in the 1954 hurricane. The farm land on both sides of the road long ago reverted back to woodland except for landscaping around newer houses. The extensive out-lying woodlots and farm lands on both sides of the Rehoboth and Dighton town line are all within the large Dighton-Rehoboth School complex. Roy Horton, who for years was the caretaker of the West Dighton cemetery, said that David W. Francis, both of his wives, and his three children are all buried in one lot in the cemetery under a large expensive monument, but Roy could not remember ever seeing anyone go near the lot or care for the graves beyond the standard perpetual care.

Another monument of sorts does exist in Rehoboth to Mr. Francis' memory but few people if any know about it today. During the first decade of this century when none of the town roads in Rehoboth had names, the selectmen were authorized at a town meeting to name all the streets. At the time Mr. Francis owned a second farm on what is now Francis Street that he had purchased in 1890 and two very large woodlots on both sides of that street near the farm. Since he had the only house on that street at that time and was also the largest land owner in that area, it was decided to name the street Francis Street after him.

FRANCIS J. WHEELER

A short distance up New Street from the David W. Francis homestead lived another operator admired by the Hortons, Francis J. Wheeler (1848-1928). Mr. Wheeler for many years ran a general farm and wood business in partnership with his father Jasper W. Wheeler (1822-1892). The Wheelers were an old family whose ancestors were among the first settlers of Rehoboth. Francis and his wife Julia (Sisson) (1851-1935) had three sons, Edward (Eddie) (1871-1921), Elkanah (1877-1925), and Henry (1874-1960). Eddie and Henry worked and lived on the farm their whole lives, but Elkanah found other employment in Taunton and later was a proprietor of a small store at Wheeler's Corner in Rehoboth. Francis met his wife Julia when attending a "kitchen dance" held at a farm on Wheeler Street, Dighton. Before the days of school dances and night clubs, young people met and socialized by attending dances held at neighboring homes, such as this one held in a kitchen. The Hall at the Horton farm sometimes was used for similar social gatherings. Since transportation was slow and difficult during the nineteenth century, it was not easy to find a husband or wife outside the local area; so marriages frequently took place between neighboring families. Francis Wheeler's sister, Elizabeth Wheeler, always called Lizzie, was David W. Francis' first wife. Their only child, Frederick Ernest Francis, mentioned earlier, was first cousin to Henry Wheeler and his best friend.

The Wheelers' hay and cultivated fields were situated along both sides of New Street and on the westerly side of Maple Swamp Road just after the first sharp bend in that road in Dighton. The Wheeler farm buildings were efficiently arranged opposite each other on both sides of New Street with the farm house in the center of the grouping. Behind the house was a rectangular two story building that served as a combination woodwork shop, tool shed, sleeping quarters, and privy. In the shop there was a bench to repair tools and a grindstone to sharpen axes and other farm implements. Over in the corner was an old cast iron cook stove that had been moved into the shop from the house after Francis had bought a beautiful new Kalamazoo cookstove for his wife. After the first of January, the shop was also used for cutting up and processing pork. The old stove was used to prepare sausage and everything else that needed cooking when slaughtering pigs. Out in the yard, Eddie was in charge of curing the hams and bacon in smoke barrels that he had fired up with corn cobs and charcoal dust. After the killing and the processing were completed, the pork, bacon, and hams were hung upstairs in the shed where they remained frozen during the winter until ready for use. Francis Wheeler's granddaughter, Pearl Wheeler Quint, who witnessed it all as a child, can still recall 75 years later how good it all smelled.

On occasion the old stove in the shed was used by Francis and his two sons Eddie and Henry to boil water in a large kettle to steam sled runners when they were being bent into their proper shapes. The shop also had an entirely different use during the growing season. The room upstairs where the hams and pork had hung during the winter became the bedroom where the hired men slept from spring through to fall. Each year the Wheelers hired extra help to work on the farm. During the early 1900's the workers were usually French Canadians who had recently immigrated to this area from Canada. Two immigrant girls from Portugal were also hired each summer to help with the additional work of caring for the hired men by waiting on tables and cooking in the kitchen. Pearl recalled that having these foreigners at the place gave the farm during the summer a sort of cosmopolitan atmosphere.

Between the Wheelers' shop and the easterly shore of Squannakonk Swamp stood a hen house surrounded by a large two acre hen yard. On the other side of New Street from the house was a barn where about 20 cows, a pair of oxen, and seven or eight work horses were kept. The barn cellar opened on the east to a good sized pig pen. Following the usual custom, the pigs lived in the barn cellar, feeding and rooting all winter

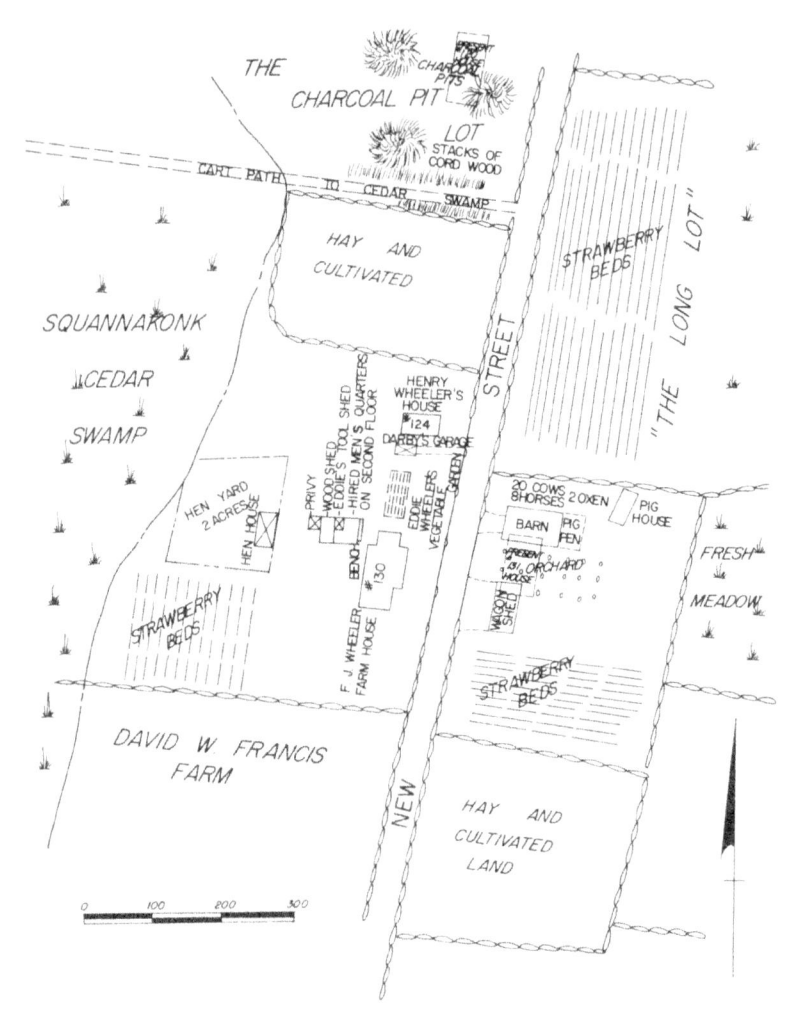

FRANCIS J. WHEELER FARM
Rehoboth, circa 1910

in the cow manure after it was dropped through scuttles in the main barn floor from above. South of the barn was a large wagon shed facing on New Street. The wagons were kept in the open faced section of the shed, but the much valued new buggy, purchased in 1910, was protected from the weather with a door. The huge specially built charcoal or coal wagon was also kept in this shed. The all important strawberry beds were situated for easy access near the house by the hen yard and also across New Street both south and north of the barn. Other strawberry beds were located on the westerly side of Maple Swamp Road in Dighton at a place called the Old Fields. At this location was the Orchard Lot where the Wheelers had a packing shed used to sort, clean, and store vegetables before delivering them at market.

Francis Wheeler had a reputation for being very particular about maintaining the quality of his farm products; the cabbage, strawberries, and other vegetables had to be perfect before marketing. Pearl remembers picking strawberries in these fields in the early 1900's for her grandfather for 2 cents per box. Each box after being filled was carefully examined to be sure there were no crushed berries. If one was found, the picker was not paid for that box. The Wheelers were equally careful and successful in operating their dairy and milk route. For a number of years their milk was taken daily by wagon to Taunton and sold wholesale to stores. Harold A. Goff, who was brought up on a dairy farm in the Perryville section of Rehoboth and later was to serve as a Rehoboth Selectman and the North Bristol County Registrar of Deeds, bought the Wheelers' milk wholesale to sell on the Goff Farm's door to door retail milk route in Pawtucket. When strawberries were in season, the Goffs often purchased at wholesale the Wheelers' strawberries to peddle on their milk route.

As important as these enterprises were, the Wheelers, like their neighbors David W. Francis and George H. Goff, found that the wood sales in Pawtucket were especially profitable during the last decades of the nineteenth century and they accordingly became an important part of their farm work. Much of their woodland was located in Squannakonk Swamp, a short distance to the rear of their house. During the winter, Eddie and Henry Wheeler along with any hired help available spent

Views of the Jasper and Francis J. Wheeler House at 130 New Street, Rehoboth.

Photograph taken in the 1890's. Henry Wheeler is holding the horse (cut off) on left; Julia Wheeler standing in back of fence, Emily Smith stading in front of gate, and Eddie Wheeler holding horse.

About 1900. Note the milk cans drying on the fence.

Same view today

much of their time in the Swamp chopping and hauling out the next year's supply of firewood. Much of it was stored on the upland along the path leading into the Swamp from New Street a little north of the Henry Wheeler house. Roy said that Jasper Wheeler, grandfather of Eddie and Henry, was considered to be an excellent woodsman. Roy, born after Jasper died, did not know him, but was told by Roy's father that Jasper was a strong man with a great deal of stamina. With his axe, he would go into Squannakonk Swamp, cut down, and chop up into four foot lengths, but not stack, seven cords of black ash in one day. Since black ash was a fairly tall tree, soft to cut and with few lower branches, the chopping was easier than with other hard woods, but that was still considered to be quite a feat and difficult to match today by a man using a chain saw. An ordinary day's work cutting maple or oak with an axe yielded one cord cut and stacked. Roy was also told by his father that Jasper could cradle rye faster than any other farmer in the area. Cradling was done with a special scythe fitted with light wooden fingers attached to the snath (handle). As the farmer swung the scythe into the rye, the cut stalks landed on the fingers from which they could be dumped in piles for easier retrieval. Roy heard that if Jasper had a little rum before beginning in the morning and a little more at noon, he would cradle like a machine all day.

Charcoal burning was another important money making enterprise for which the Wheelers were noted. The Wheelers' charcoal pits were located on the west side of New Street, a little north of the Wheeler house where Vincent Cavallaro now lives at 120 New Street. Charcoal had been burned at this site from the earliest days of the settlement of Rehoboth. During the nineteenth century charcoal was in great demand by the numerous blacksmith shops and foundries in the area. For many years the Taunton State Hospital was an important customer of the Wheelers.

The charcoal burning was done at three pits at the Cavallaro site. Well seasoned wood that had been cut the year before was stacked in a rick to make a pile about 25 feet by 25 feet and covered with charcoal dust and earth. The wood was set on fire but only allowed to smolder by the regulation of the oxygen supply through a hole punched in the earth at the base of the pile. If the fire broke through the earth wall, it had to be extin-

Julia Wheeler

Jasper Wheeler

THE WHEELER FAMILY

Francis J. Wheeler in front of his barn.

Francis J. Wheeler, Julia Wheeler, and Jeff in 1923 on the farmhouse front porch.

Edward F. Wheeler, Elkanah Wheeler, and Henry Walker Wheeler, circa 1887.

guished immediately or the whole stack of wood within a short time would be reduced to a pile of worthless ashes. When there was such a "fire flare out," an attendant climbed up on top of the pit on a ladder and stuffed an armful of wet corn husks in the burning hole. This was dangerous work, because if the man slipped off the ladder and broke through the earth, he would land in a mass of fiery hot burning embers. For years Walter Wheeler (no relation) of Winthrop Street, Dighton, performed this task. After Walter was killed by a street car not far from his home near the Segregansett Country Club, Henry Wheeler, father of Pearl, was given that job. Pearl still remembers how worried she was that something would happen to her father when he was on top of the burning piles. It took about five days for a rick of wood to be rendered into charcoal, during which time an attendant had to be there day and night to supervise the burning pits. When automobiles became common, people from Taunton and other surrounding towns often drove out to see and enjoy the aroma of the burning pits. After the charcoal had cooled, the earth was removed and the charcoal was sifted and graded in wooden basketlike sieves and delivered to customers in the large Wheeler coal wagon. People also came to the farm and bought charcoal packed in burlap bags from the Wheelers.

Pearl never knew her grandfather Jasper, having been born after his death, but she recalls an amusing story the Wheelers used to tell about Jasper and his son Francis. Father and son got along well working on the farm together except when it came to politics. Jasper was a strong Democrat, while Francis was an equally strong supporter of the Republican party. Election day reminded the father of this difference between them; so when they went to the polls to vote, Jasper absolutely refused to ride with his son and they each rode in separate buggies. Jasper's intention was to make it as difficult as possible for his son to get to the polls so as not to cancel out his vote.

Another of Francis Wheeler's business enterprises was begun shortly after the trolley line connecting the cities of Taunton and Providence along Winthrop Street in Rehoboth (present Route 44) was finished in 1899. The eight or ten mile trip to Taunton or Providence from Rehoboth was reduced by the trolley to about 20 or 30 minutes in contrast to a two hour bumpy ride with a horse and wagon. Besides carrying passengers, the Street Railway Company ran local freight cars over the tracks both morning and evenings. The corner of New Street and Winthrop Street became an important stopping place for both passengers and freight. To take advantage of this new development, Mr. Wheeler built at his own expense on the northeast corner of those streets a depot containing a waiting room for passengers and a storage area for freight articles. The station was illuminated with electric bulbs supplied with power from the trolley line. Besides this building, the car barn, Goff Memorial Hall, and George N. Goff's house, all in Rehoboth Village, were probably the only buildings in Rehoboth with electric illumination, all supplied with power by the street railway company. Mr. Wheeler was hired by the Street Railway Company to be their freight agent, not a full time job, but carried on only when a freight shipment or customers were expected. Besides shipping and receiving freight items for the local farmers, Mr. Wheeler used the depot to store and sell fertilizer for a company he had become an agent for. All this activity was in addition to his other enterprises of dairy and vegetable farming and the preparation and sale of charcoal and firewood. Because of all this activity here by the Wheeler family, the corner soon began to be called Wheeler's Corner, by which name it is still know today.

According to Roy, Francis J. Wheeler accumulated considerable money and property from all these activities. By the time he died in 1928, however, he had lost most of it and his estate was insolvent. The farm and many woodlots that he owned were sold at auction by the Probate Court. Some said his financial misfortune was caused by his long last illness. He had suffered from cancer of the face. Others said the misfortune was caused by the way he catered to the two sons who remained with him on the farm, Eddie and Henry. According to Pearl, daughter of Henry, "Francis Wheeler's problem was that he loved his children too much." Unlike his neighbor David W. Francis, he had a great family life and did everything he could to make his sons' lives easier. Roy remembered that Eddie owned and managed a large flock of poultry on the Wheeler farm. Since Francis bought all the grain for his son's enterprise and never charged for it, Eddie could not help but make a profit. For Henry he built and gave the house which still stands at 126 New Street. According to Roy, both sons had it easy, but perhaps Eddie was more of the worker. Eddie died at age 50, another victim of appendicitis, and had never married. I can see the two brothers now, recalled Roy, Eddie sitting in the center of the wagon seat, going down New Street with his brother Henry always standing in the back. Henry never sat down and Eddie always took up a full seat. They would be most likely on their way to the vegetable packing shed on Maple Swamp Road in Dighton.

The house built for Henry W. Wheeler by Francis J. Wheeler at 126 New Street, Rehoboth.

Perhaps the reason Eddie was able to do more physical work than his brother was due to a freak and almost tragic accident that Henry experienced when a youth. In 1890 when he was 16 years old he was in the woods chopping trees for his father when a tree "kicked back," fell on his leg, and caused a severe compound fracture. Henry was brought to the Wheeler farm house and a doctor was summoned. The doctor performed the operation to repair the fracture not in the hospital, but on the Wheeler dining room table. Pearl Quint, who at age 12 went to live with her grandparents, Francis and Julia Wheeler, recalls hearing over and over how during the operation the smell of ether was so strong you could smell it out in the yard. Henry eventually recovered but always walked with a limp for the rest of his life. The doctor removed a piece of bone which Henry kept as a souvenier for the rest of his life. Pearl remembers that even though a little crippled, Henry always tried to carry his share of the load when farm work needed to be done.

Farming was and still is considered one of the more hazardous occupations. Francis Wheeler, like his son, also suffered

E. Otis Dyer shells corn with a corn sheller from the Francis J. Wheeler Farm.

a serious accident on the farm. When chopping up feed for his pigs on one very cold morning, he cut off two of his fingers on his left hand without knowing it. He said his hand was so cold that he did not feel it and did not know what had happened until he saw blood on top of the skimmed milk that he was preparing for the pigs. To stop the bleeding he used an old home remedy; from a corner in the barn he gathered all the cobweb he could find, placed it over his severed fingers, and wrapped the hand with a milk strainer cloth. Later his son, Elkanah, drove him in the buggy to a doctor in Taunton for further treatment. For some time his two sons Eddie and Henry had to do all the farm chores. After the hand healed, he suffered no really crippling effects.

As in the case of the old Francis farm, little can be seen today of the extensive farm and wood and charcoal activities once carried on by the Wheelers. The old Wheeler homestead still stands at 130 New Street as does the house next door which Francis Wheeler built for his son Henry at 126 New Street. Where tons of cordwood were rendered into charcoal over the years by the Wheelers stands the Cavallaro house at 120 New Street. The barn on the east side of New Street has been gone for 50 years but portions of the wagon shed still stood into the 1960's. House #131 is now on or near those sites. The Wheeler farm and most of the wood lots were sold at auction shortly after Francis' death in 1928 to satisfy his estate creditors. The farm land that has not been divided into house lots has entirely reverted back to woodland.

GEORGE HATHAWAY GOFF

Another New Street wood operator was George Hathaway Goff (1848-1903) who owned a large farm of about 160 acres on both sides of New Street north of the Wheeler farm, near Wheeler's Corner and running easterly into Dighton along both sides of Maple Swamp Road. This was the farm where Roy left his bicycle for the day while attending Taunton High School. At the time Roy was familiar with the farm, Mr. Goff had been dead for a number of years and the farm was being operated by his oldest son, Arthur H. Goff. Like David W. Francis, George H. Goff had been active in the firewood business during its best days in the latter decades of the nineteenth century. He was as successful, if not more so, than Mr. Francis in this enterprise and by the time of his untimely death at age 55 in 1903, he had accumulated a great deal of property including many wood lots to supply wood for his firewood and charcoal business. Also, like Mr. Francis, he reinvested much of the profits he made in these enterprises into the form of loans and mortgages to his neighbors. In 1903 he had over $6,000.00 invested in this manner out of a total of almost $22,000.00 he owned in other investments. Some of his other holdings were over $11,000.00 in local savings banks, $1,000.00 in dairy cows, $400.00 in horses, $200.00 in oxen, along with large investments in wagons, harnesses, charcoal tools, hay, strawberry crates, turnips, and potatoes. At this time (1903) his 160 acres farm was valued at $6,000.00 and his 25 wood lots scattered about East Rehoboth and West Dighton, like the George A. Case Lot, George Wheeler Lot, Hicks Meadow, Rocky Hill Carpenter Lot, Great Meadow Hill Carpenter Lot, Cushing Swamp, Hicks Swamp, Polly Goff Lot, Joanna Horton Lot, Otis Nichols Lot, and Elephant Meadow, all were valued at $2,000.00. (See Appendix V)

It would be of interest after allowing for the inflation that has occurred over the past ninety years to compare the value of the wealth Mr. Goff was able to accumulate from his various enterprises in a rural setting and economy with today's prices. This is very difficult to do because of the extensive depreciation of the dollar since 1903. One comparison, however, may be made by using the relative values of a working wage, then and now. According to Roy Horton, a laborer in 1903 was able to

George Hathaway Goff House at 66 New Street, Rehoboth, circa 1910.

Same view today.

chop and stack about one cord of wood per day for $1.00 to $1.50. If he was able to perform this task without interference from inclement weather, his weekly wage would have been $5.00 to $7.00 for a five day week. Today if someone could be hired to do the same type of work with a chain saw, his pay, perhaps, would be $400.00 per week or more, thus giving an average ratio between the two rates of pay of about seventy to one. This ratio would make Mr. Goff's personal property (mortgages, loans, bank accounts, cows, etc.) which was valued about $22,000.00 in 1903 worth about $1,540,000.00 today. Because of my own familiarity as a surveyor with much of the real estate Mr. Goff once owned, I am able to give a fairly accurate estimate of its worth in today's market. During the 1960's I divided Mr. Goff's 160 acre farm into twelve house lots, having a present day value of about three quarters of a million dollars. The remaining farm acreage, farm house, barn (still standing), and 25 wood lots are probably worth in today's prices a third of a million, making Mr. Goff if he were still alive well over a multi-millionaire. However, no matter how the Goffs' and other operators' property is analyzed, in either today's or the turn of the century's prices, it remains quite an accomplishment for them to have amassed that much wealth in a depressed economy and in a rural environment. Most people living then, as Roy often said, were lucky to make ends meet. However, unlike David Francis, George H. Goff was able to be a business success and still keep the respect of his neighbors and the love of his children and wife.

Besides the firewood, dairy, and vegetable business, enterprises common to many other farmers in Rehoboth and Dighton, Goff, like Francis J. Wheeler, also carried on a successful charcoal enterprise. Cordwood cut from his numerous wood lots by his hired men was rendered into charcoal at his charcoal pits and sold to blacksmiths and foundries locally and in the neighboring cities. Some of these pits were located at the rear of his farm along the old abandoned road leading toward Winthrop Street; other sites were on the south side of Winthrop Street about where house #23 is now located. At least two of his charcoal sites have been recently discovered deep in the woods in the vicinity of Great Meadow Hill. One is on the north side of the hill a little south of the East Branch of the Palmer River on

An exterior and interior view of one of the barns at the George Hathaway Goff Farm at 66 New Street, Rehoboth as it looks today. Note the horse looking at us from his stall.

property owned by the author and the other is near the top of the hill in the State Forest. Traces of charcoal can be still found in the sod at both of these sites, some of which are remarkably preserved.

On January 24, 1903, Mr. Goff suffered a fatal accident. He had taken his horse and buggy into Taunton, about eight miles away from his farm, on a business errand. Returning home after dark about 9:00 P.M., his buggy collided with a large freight wagon owned by the Taunton Teaming Company, being driven by Alexander Russell, at the foot of Goodings Hill on Winthrop Street, Dighton, about where the Segregansett Country Club is situated. The *Taunton Daily Gazette* gave the following account of the accident:

> He [Russell] was coming from Providence and when near Westville [a village in West Taunton] he saw a light carriage coming toward him at quite a high rate of speed. He called to the other driver and pulled out of the way as far as possible, but the occupant of the carriage either did not hear him or could not clear the heavier wagon and ran directly into Russell's wagon. The [Goff] horse cleared itself and ran on, but the man [Mr. Goff] was thrown into the road with great force and lay as one dead. Russell immediately went to him, but he [Goff] was insensible although [Russell] stated to the police that he could discover no cuts or evidence of broken bones.
>
> Mr. Goff was picked up and carried to the nearby house of the greenskeeper, Joseph Olson, at the Segregansett Country Club; Mr. Russell continued on to Taunton where he notified the police. Russell, when he returned to the scene of the accident, met Mr. Goff's son, Arthur H. Goff, who told him that a Mr. Joseph Olson had carried Mr. Goff to his home [Goff Farm] and that he was then on the way to Taunton to find a physician, there being no phones at the Goff farm. The Goff family knew before Mr. Olson appeared at the Goff Farm with Mr. Goff that something had happened to their father, because the Goff horse had already arrived in the dooryard without the buggy, the horse having bolted from the accident scene and

run home. Despite the care of a doctor, Mr. Goff never gained consciousness and died three days later at his home, leaving a wife and nine children, the four youngest being minor.

Arthur H. Goff, the eldest son, had farmed at various times at what is now the Schobel farm on Anawan Street in Rehoboth, at a farm later to be owned by Lester Waterman on the corner of New Street and County Street, and also at a farm just over the town line in Dighton on the north side of Winthrop Street. The latter farm was his home at the time of his father's death. Arthur and his family moved to the Goff home on New Street soon after the accident to continue the Goff business operations. In this endeavor, Arthur was not very successful and by the time he died in 1930 little was left on the large Goff holdings. Not only was Arthur not the business man that his father was, but he also had the additional disadvantage of trying to carry on the wood business in a rapidly declining firewood and charcoal market. Arthur was probably the last person to make charcoal in Rehoboth. Horace Smith, (1902-1992) who married Arthur's granddaughter, recalled around 1924 tending a charcoal pit during the night watch at about where house number #23 on Winthrop Street is now located. Horace recalls that Mr. Goff would stack up six or eight cords of wood and cover them with earth and sod. As the pile smoldered over several days it was Horace's job to stay up all night to be sure the fire only smoldered. If it flared up, he had to cover up the fire quickly with more sod or wet corn stalks.

Another charcoal burning site often used by Arthur H. Goff

was southerly off Fairview Avenue on the west border of the Ash Swamp Lot. These charcoal burning pits are now on the property owned by Leo and Muriel Zuckerberg. The Ash Swamp was a large maple swamp that extended northerly from Winthrop Street to Fairview Avenue. It was not only a source of cordwood for the Goff charcoal pits, but also used by the Stiles and Hart Brick Company in Taunton which owned a large tract in the swamp. Here the Company cut cordwood to fire its brick making kilns off Hart and Plain Street in Taunton. As Mr. Goff made less and less charcoal at his pits, he became more of a dealer or middleman in charcoal which he imported from other parts of the country over the railroads.

Horace remembered that he was often hired by Mr. Goff to unload into a Goff wagon the charcoal from railroad cars delivered in three bushel burlap bags at the Taunton freight yard and then to bring it directly to factories in Taunton and Attleboro for use in their foundries and machine shops; Reed and Barton Silversmiths of Taunton were large users of this product.

The wagon shed at the Goff Farm is leaning but still standing.

Another business enterprise that took place at the Goff farm during these years was the operation of a home delivery dairy serving the Taunton area. The dairy was owned and operated by Christopher J. Varley, who married Arthur's daughter Grace. Christopher, Grace, and their family shared the farm house with Arthur and his wife. A bottling plant was set up by Mr. Varley in a vacant shed at the rear of the Goff farm building on the right side of the old abandoned road (Old Winthrop Street) running toward Rehoboth. The milk produced from the Goff cows supplied milk to the Varley dairy. Other farmers also sold milk here wholesale, including at one time Henry W. Horton and his son Raymond. This dairy processed and delivered milk door to door in Taunton from 1918 to 1930; it too had to close its doors as did so many small dairies at the beginning of the Great Depression. After the closing of the dairy and the death of Arthur Goff, the farm was soon sold to Elwood Horton, Roy's older brother. Elwood ran it as a dairy farm until his death in 1964.

After Elwood's death in 1964, the Hortons divided what were once the Goff pastures and hay and strawberry fields on both sides of New Street and Maple Swamp Road into a number of house lots, transforming the farm into a small suburban neighborhood. The only evidence that can be seen today of the once extensive Goff business activities are the old farm house, the two barns, and a wagon shed that still stand on some substantial acreage kept with the original farm. No farming activity except for the stabling of a riding house takes place here today. Much of the remaining acreage is now overgrown with brush.

SAMUEL E. SMITH

An operator who would be classified as a minor player in the wood business when compared to those just mentioned, even though he was very ambitious and hard working, was Samuel E. Smith, (1866 -1945). Samuel Smith lived with his wife Ruth and their five sons, Samuel S., Elisha, Byron, Horace E., and John B. Smith at what is now 46 Francis Street in Rehoboth. It was David Francis who sold the farm to the Smiths in 1906. Francis originally purchased the place in 1890 as a second farm. Sam Smith, as he was generally called, in the tradition of the other operators milked about 20 cows as his everyday work and cut and sold firewood as a major supplementary business.

Today, much of the Francis Street area of Rehoboth and particularly the top and slopes of Great Meadow Hill, the highest elevation in Rehoboth, are covered with a vast hardwood forest. However, this heavy growth of wood was not always there. Portions of the Hill were cleared for crops and pastures in earlier times as proven by numerous stone walls — always an indicator that the land was once pastured or tilled. It has been said that during the early decades of the nineteenth century if a person stood on Francis Street at the foot of the Hill and gazed up the slope, he would see the summit covered with a corn field shimmering and waving in the wind. This corn would have been growing on the land owned by John Davis, an earlier owner of the Smith farm, and was known by him as his Hill Field.

Other accounts say that Joseph McCormick, a contractor from East Providence, in later years each summer drove out a herd of cattle to pasture on the Hill. As the land lost its fertility and became brushy, sheep also were grazed there. This practice is verified not only by local tradition, but by the water hole at the East Branch of the Palmer River at the foot of the north slope of the Hill, known as the *sheep hole*. Here sheep were driven to be washed before shearing. Also a stone wall still standing not far from Fairview Avenue part way up on the west side of the Hill (the west terrace) was built in such a way that sheep could be herded into an area where converging walls funneled them into a stone holding pen. No doubt this structure was also used in the fall to gather the cattle as well as sheep

GREAT MEADOW HILL
Rehoboth, circa 1900

that had pastured there during the summer, always a difficult task after a summer of freedom. One section of the west side of the Hill on the terrace was used as an apple orchard during the middle 1800's. This elevated site was chosen to protect the early blossoms from a late frost. Cold air has a tendency to slide down a hill and collect in the low lying areas.

As the Hill grew back into woods after the Civil War, paths that were used for access to the various lots were kept open and were used by the Smiths, Francis, and others to haul out firewood and timber to the roads. One well defined path was on the west terrace. This path began at Fairview Avenue and ran northerly the whole length of the side of the Hill, then over a fording place and bridge at the East Branch of the Palmer River out to what is now Billings Road. Another major path also began at Fairview Avenue and ran westerly over the top of the Hill and joined the first mentioned path near the river. From near that junction another path ran northeasterly out to Peck Street. A branch of that path entered Francis Street north of the Samuel Smith farm. Segments of paths ran to and along the bottom of the Hill to allow access to the fresh meadow lots in the large marsh known as the Great Meadow, an area that gave Great Meadow Hill its name. An excellent path ran from the end of what is now Billings Road northeasterly across another location on the river to Peck Street. At this last river crossing there was, at the turn of this century, a crude bridge strong enough to support a wagon or sled fully loaded with cord wood. Samuel S. Smith had a vivid memory from his boyhood days of seeing a heavily loaded wagon with a driver on top of the logs being pulled by four horses, hitched not in tandem, but placed one in front of the other in a row, crossing that bridge at almost a gallop. "The nicest thing you ever wanted to see," he recalled 60 years later.

The Smith farm backed up from Francis Street on to the easterly slope of the Great Meadow Hill, giving the family access to a vast source of firewood. At the time the Smiths resided here during the first decades of this century, their house was the only house on that long stretch of Francis Street. There was no electricity or telephone service; so to pick up mail, the Smiths had to walk a half mile round trip to a mail drop-off point at the Everett Short house at the present 107 Peck Street at the head of Francis Street. When the frost came out of the ground in the spring of the year, Francis Street turned into a quagmire of mud because of its poor surface. Horace Smith (1909-1992) recalled that when he was a teenager, he was often called to use his father's horse to pull out of the mud the cars of motorists who had dared venture down that street. Fairview Avenue on the east side of Great Meadow Hill was often in the spring time in equally bad condition and so badly cut up by vehicles, recalled Horace, that the teamsters preferred to use a private cart path up the Hill that ran sort of parallel to Fairview Avenue. This path began on Francis Street where house number 68 now stands and ended on the top of the Hill on what is now known as Fire Tower Road.

Since no electricity was available at the Smith farm, the refrigeration of milk during the summer months was always a problem. An attempt was made to keep it cool by storing the milk in ten quart cans and hanging them on chains down in the well. However, milk did not stay at the farm very long because each morning the Smiths carted their milk to a pickup point at the corner of Peck Street and Anawan Street in Rehoboth where along with other locally produced milk it was delivered to a dairy in Attleboro, a small city about eight miles away. Horace recalls how one day he saw a representative of the dairy come to the Smith farm and say to his father, "your milk is getting a little close to water," thus accusing the Smiths of watering down their milk. There was a dispute and after further investigation, it was found that the pickup man, while he was on his way to Attleboro with the Smith milk, would open up the cans, remove the cream, and replace it with water. Even though it was determined that the Smiths were innocent, Horace remembers his father was so angry over the accusation that he stopped dealing with the Attleboro dairy and began selling his milk to the Wade Dairy at Wade's Corner at the corner of Winthrop Street and Burt Street in Taunton and eventually ended up, like so many other farmers did, selling it to the Charles C. Marble Dairy on Williams Street, Dighton.

Although dairying was an important part of the Smith family income, their energy and interest were chiefly directed toward cutting and selling firewood. Mr. Smith soon became a large scale operator, but without the profits some of the previous generation had enjoyed in that business. However, for over twenty years until after the end of World War I, enough people were still using wood for fuel so that a decent profit could be made. Each year, the Smiths cut about 500 cords, all with the ax, and sold wood from the stacked piles to various customers or by delivery to the Olney and Paine Company, fuel dealers, in Pawtucket. The employees of Olney and Paine cut up and split the four foot lengths of wood into stove size and sold them to Pawtucket residents in bushel baskets. Horace recalls that both his father and brothers worked hard in the wood business along with hired wood cutters. The latter were paid by the Smiths at the rate of $1.00 to $1.25 per cord cut and stacked in the woods. Wood cut on the western upper slopes of the Hill was generally drawn out by horse teams over the path on the west terrace and stacked along Fairview Avenue about halfway up the west side of the Hill. Sometimes there would be hundreds of cords of wood and newly cut railroad ties stored along that road, waiting to be sold or carted to the wood yard in Pawtucket and the latter to the Street Railway Company.

Just as Henry W. Horton had the contract to supply all the Dighton schools with stove wood, Sam Smith had the same for the one room schools in North Rehoboth. Another contract the Smiths obtained was to furnish all the railway ties to the owners of the Eastern Massachusetts Street Railway who operated the trolley line running on Winthrop street through Dighton and Rehoboth. These ties were cut from the chestnut trees that were then very plentiful on Great Meadow Hill. Towards the end of World War I these beautiful trees were beginning to die from the blight that eventually destroyed them all. Chestnut was a very prized wood, straight grained and easy to split and work with. Structurally it was sound and very resistant to rot, making it well suited for fence posts, rails, railroad ties, and telephone poles. In addition to all those qualities it was an excellent firewood.

Horace remembers his family cutting chestnut all over the Hill during the winter of 1917 to supply the street railroad contract. The chestnut trees were felled and cut up into railroad tie lengths by the Smith wood cutters. Everett Short, a neighbor who lived on a farm at the corner of Peck Street and Francis Street, did all the hewing of the ties for the Smiths, right where

Samuel Smith as a conductor of the horse car trolleys in Pawtucket, circa 1890.

Samuel Smith in later years standing in his doorway with his sister-in-law and his five boys, Horace, Byron, John, Elisha, Sammy, circa 1918.

the trees had fallen. After the ties had been hewn smoothly on two sides by Mr. Short, the Smith boys were given the job of carting them through the brush out to the nearest cart path. The ties were too heavy for two boys to pick up; so one brother would shove a stick under the upper third of the tie over to another brother. The two boys would then lift the stick and raise the tie off the ground while a third brother held up and steadied the load at the rear. Horace recalls that hundreds of ties were moved that winter in this manner out to the cart path and later hauled by teams to Fairview Avenue for stacking. Eventually from there they were hauled to the street railway freight depot at Wheeler's Corner where they were again stacked in preparation for transportation by the trolley freight cars to the company storage yard in Taunton.

In 1914, when Horace was five years old, a fire tower was built by the state on the top of Great Meadow Hill. It was located a little south of where a signal beacon had stood during the Revolution. When the British occupied Newport, Rhode Island, on a number of occasions they threatened to raid the countryside towards Rehoboth and neighboring towns. For a warning system these towns set up a chain of observation points and beacons to call up the Minute Men when a British troop movement was detected. Rehoboth had an observation post on the corner of Brook and Chestnut Streets looking southwest. When a beacon fire was seen burning down towards Barrington, Rhode Island, a man on horseback would immediately be sent riding across town to light Rehoboth's beacon to warn the militia of the towns to the north.

Horace recalled that the general contractor for the fire tower was John Crane whose workers sometimes lived and boarded at the Smith house while working on the project. On one occasion, Horace Smith recalled how important he felt when he was asked to climb the Hill to deliver a lunch to one of the workmen.

The Smiths were not the only wood operators cutting on Great Meadow Hill during the first decade of this century. Although advanced in years, David W. Francis was still active and from 1900 to 1910 cut off a large tract of land he owned on the southeast side of the Hill. Howard P. Lovecraft (1890-1936), a famous writer of supernatural stories, on a visit to the top of the Hill in 1909 noted, "the new cut off forest... gave us a vast horizon and panorama." H. P. Lovecraft at the time was a youth living in Providence. He and some friends during a bicycle excursion to Rehoboth in 1907 found an abandoned wood cutter's cabin on what is now the west side of Fire Tower Road near the summit of the Hill. Impressed with the beauty of the setting, they decided to convert the shack into a clubhouse. In order to make it usable during the colder months, they employed a wood cutter, Civil War veteran James McKay who was living nearby, to help them build a stone fireplace and chimney at one end of the clubhouse. The newly refurbished structure was named by the boys The Great Meadow Country Club.

Upon returning to the site with a friend 15 years later H. P. Lovecraft discovered much to his surprise that aside from a broken lock, nothing had been disturbed in the clubhouse over all those years; even the table and pictures on the wall were still there, not a pane of glass was broken, and the tar paper was still on the roof and walls. However, unknown to Lovecraft, the clubhouse had not remained unused all those years. During an interview in 1975 Samuel S. Smith said, "I was going to school — age 13 or 14. We found a cabin atop of Great Meadow Hill, abandoned, no life around it. We would go up there sometimes in the evening and have parties. It was said Brown College boys built it. We never disturbed anything they had left. We used lanterns [kerosene] and picked up some dead wood to use in the fireplace." Until the Smiths were told about Lovecraft 60 years later, they had no idea what a famous personage was associated with the cabin.

In this very rural and isolated part of Rehoboth there were few recreational activities in those days for the Smith boys. The occasional party at the Great Meadow Country Club was one favorite pastime; another was hunting. Mr. Smith and his boys enjoyed hunting fox and raccoons. They raised hounds for this purpose. The woodlands of Great Meadow Hill were a favorite habitat of the red fox and raccoons. There were fox dens near the summit of the Hill and at the foot of the north slope overlooking the East Branch of the Palmer River. Since a fox generally runs in a big circle when being trailed by the hounds, the hunter must guess where on his trail the fox will return and then wait hidden until the fox appears. In contrast, raccoons are driven through the woods at night by the hounds with hunters running behind with lights fastened on their caps to light the way. When closely pressed by the dogs, the coon usually runs up a tree and is held there by the jumping hounds until the hunters appear. John Smith one night in February, 1932, killed a coon weighing 20 lbs. on the hill near Fairview Avenue. Mrs. Smith prepared the coon for supper and invited a number of friends over to enjoy a coon dinner, another favorite pastime of rural Rehoboth families of that period.

It seems that anyone who works long enough in the woods, either with an ax or chain saw, sooner or later suffers an accident. When Horace was in his late teens, he and two of his brothers were sent by their father to the Big Back Pasture at the rear of the Smith farm at the foot of Great Meadow Hill to cut wood. There was no snow, but the ground was covered with ice from a freezing rain during the night. As Horace swung his ax at the base of a tree, his foot slipped, missed the tree completely, and the razor sharp blade sliced deeply and lengthwise into the lower part of his left leg just above the ankle. His two brothers assisted him home by crossing their wrists in such a way as to make a seat for Horace to ride on. Mr. Smith immediately went to the nearest phone which was at Wheeler's Corner and called Dr. Butler in Taunton for medical assistance. The doctor quickly responded and boarded the next trolley car leaving for Rehoboth. Mr. Smith was waiting for him at the corner and drove him to the farm in his wagon. The operation to repair the wound, just as after Henry Wheeler's accident some 25 years before, was done not in a hospital but in the Smiths' house, but in this case no anesthesia was used. Horace remembers that the doctor sewed up the gash with tight stitches, using a heavy white thread on a big needle. The tight stitches helped pull the bone together where it had been split. The needle and thread were so heavy that the doctor needed pliers to pull through the stitches. Horace was told by the doctor that the ax had almost gone completely through his leg; a quarter inch more and it would have appeared on the back side of his leg. Horace was a long time recovering from his accident, and for the rest of his life the large scar and deformed bone could still be clearly seen on his leg.

Like Roy, Horace was given the task at the age of 13 of

hauling his father's cordwood to the Olney and Paine Company in Pawtucket. This was done in a large wagon drawn by two horses, loaded with two cords plus two feet of wood (two and one quarter cords) stacked in three foot tiers per load. Unlike earlier times when Emerson Goff hauled wood to the same place for David W. Francis, now, around 1922 and after, no throngs of people desperate to buy wood to heat their houses met Horace in the streets. There was still some demand for stove wood, but cheap kerosene was rapidly putting an end to the use of wood as a main source of heating fuel.

The Smith wood business did continue over the next two decades, but with diminishing demand, and it finally ended in 1945 at the time of the death of Sam Smith. Horace recalled that about that time he was asked by his mother to haul out of the woods to the side of Peck Street the wood that had been cut on the Robert White lot. Mrs. Smith had a buyer and needed the money. This was not only the last of the Smiths' wood business, but it probably was one of the last large sales in Rehoboth and Dighton for the next 30 years until firewood again became popular during the OPEC oil embargo and fuel shortage in the 1970's. The woodlands of Rehoboth and Dighton benefited from this long interval when cheap oil was available for fuel. It gave the trees time to recover from the continual cutting that had taken place from when the forest was originally cleared off in the early part of the eighteenth century on up to the 1920's. Horace recalls that when his family was the most active in the wood business during the first two decades of this century, there was still a considerable number of trees on Great Meadow Hill that were of good size and up to 40 to 60 years old, in sharp contrast to what Roy experienced while cutting during that same period in the swamps with his father. Roy noted that the forest had been cut over so often that the wood was of all small diameter and rarely required splitting. This finding is further verified by the pictures of that era which invariably show a pile of wood on a cart or sled or a stack by a dooryard of a house to be all of small size. Perhaps Great Meadow Hill where the Smiths did most of their cutting was not cut so heavily because it was in a remote part of town and steep slopes made access to some lots difficult.

Before the removal of the fire tower and the construction of the Nike Base, the top of Great Meadow Hill was always a favorite recreational place for the townspeople to visit, particularly when the fire tower was in operation. After a dizzying climb up the open steel stairs, the congenial forest-warden always invited the visitors inside his spotting cabin. From here the visitor had a beautiful panoramic view of Rehoboth and surrounding towns. Even long before the tower was built and H.P. Lovecraft discovered the beauty of the site, earlier residents of the town also appreciated a visit and a picnic here. The following account appeared in the *Rehoboth Townsman Newspaper* of July 9, 1887 of such a visit: "On the Fourth of July people in the vicinity of Meadow Hill participated in a picnic in a grove on top of the above named hill. The occasion passed off pleasantly and was enjoyed by old and young. The company numbered about fifty."

Horace Smith (1909-1992) at age 80 still doing what he enjoyed most, cutting and stacking firewood.

PART 3

IMPRESSIONS AND REFLECTIONS

The pastures are full of ghosts for me, the morning woods full of angels. Now and then they give me a broad hint.
Ralph Waldo Emerson

Recent views of the Horton barn, Wellington Street, West Dighton, after being rebuilt into a horse stable.

Chapter I

THE NEIGHBORHOOD TODAY

As I look over the West Dighton and East Rehoboth scene almost 100 years after Roy's birth, I like to reflect on the changes that have occurred. Although Perry's Corner at the intersection of County and New Street in the heart of Roy's neighborhood is only about ten miles from downtown Providence and approximately equally distant from the centers of the Massachusetts cities of Attleboro, Taunton, and Fall River, the countryside still has a rural appearance, or perhaps it may better be described as rural suburbia. Urban sprawl associated with most all metropolitan areas never reached the West Dighton and East Rehoboth area to any great degree, mainly because the numerous nearby Rhode Island residents preferred not to live in Massachusetts either out of habit or because of the difference between Massachusetts and Rhode Island taxes. Also the nearby Massachusetts cities have had generally depressed economies for many years. Since the textile industries began to migrate south 75 years ago, their growth has been slow and have had little impact on Rehoboth and Dighton.

Another reason the two towns have not experienced the rapid expansion of other communities is that no major interstate highway has yet been built through either of the towns, except for Route 195 that crosses the southeast corner of Rehoboth. So far, this highway has not caused any great increase in the spread of population into Rehoboth, perhaps because Rehoboth has such strict zoning and environmental laws and because the route is mostly through salt marsh where much of the land is non-buildable.

In 1970, Interstate highway 895 was planned to connect Route 195 in Swansea with Route 495 in Norton. The new road would have passed through the West Dighton or the East

Rehoboth neighborhood in the vicinity of New Street. One proposed location had the road traversing the length of Squannakonk Swamp and across Bad Luck Swamp. By the time this proposal came up for serious consideration, people had become much more aware of the environment and the damage such a highway might do to the life style of the area's residents and ecological systems. Political opposition to the project became so great in Rehoboth and Dighton and other impacted towns that the State abandoned the whole project, at least temporarily.

Today, the rural suburbia look of the West Dighton and East Rehoboth neighborhood is of scattered houses situated on large lots along old country roads such as New Street, Reservoir Avenue, Smith Street, and Horton Street. Almost all the old farm houses Roy remembered as a boy still stand. Many are occupied by the descendants of families who have lived in the same houses for 100 to 200 years ago or still live nearby. The only new plat type housing is at Fieldstone Drive in the area between Smith Street and Wellington Street on the Paul-Horton farm along what was the old Paul Lane where Roy once drove the cows to Smith Street.

Most residents of the neighborhood now make their living by working in the nearby cities; agriculture has been entirely abandoned on the commercial level and only a few backyard-type part time farms remain. In a few places hay is still cut on the more improved land on the old farms, but in general the once open landscape is now heavily forested. It is impressive when one looks over the wooded scene today, keeping in mind the extent that farming once took place here, to appreciate how rapidly a Massachusetts forest can reclaim abandoned farm land. It now takes considerable imagination to visualize what the David W. Francis, Francis J. Wheeler, and the Samuel E. Smith farms once looked like. The Paul-Horton and the George Hathaway Goff farms, that were commercially farmed up to about twenty five years ago, still have some openness about them. On these latter two farms the old dairy barns still stand. The Horton barn had so badly deteriorated that portions seemed ready to collapse. Just in time, Thomas Horton, great grandson of Henry W. Horton, made extensive repairs. The barn is now fully restored and used as a horse boarding stable.

Chapter II

THE SWAMPS TODAY

It is always enjoyable for me to visit the swamps and woodlands of easterly Rehoboth, either to survey property lines or just to explore. Sometimes I search for features mentioned in old deeds like a specially mentioned property corner, stream, path, island, the remains of an old wood cutter's cabin, the outline of where a charcoal pit was once situated, or any other evidence of past activities in these places. I find the swamps to be particularly relevant and challenging in my search for signs of the activities that I know had once taken place there during the nineteenth and early decades of the twentieth century. Because the last serious wood cutting took place there 50 or more years ago, almost all signs of these activities have been obliterated by the new growth of brush, briars, and trees. The dominant red or swamp maple has grown quite large — particularly in Squannakonk Swamp. In places the underbrush and bull briars are so thick that walking is impossible without cutting out a path. Because these swamps have been avoided by people for so many years, I find them now to be quite tranquil places far removed from the hustle and bustle of the present life going on around them.

Roy was never able to accompany me into the swamps because of the difficult terrain and his lame knee, but he often patiently tried to give me directions to find what I was looking for. Once Roy was able to walk with me on the path leading out into Squannakonk Neck from Maple Lane to the edge of the swamp. He pointed out to me the right of way set off for the benefit of the swamp owners, originally laid out in the eighteenth century by Colonel Thomas Carpenter, and a bypass path with fewer stones that he had often used to make an easier drive to the swamp in a truck or old car (this was the path Roy took when he drove to the swamp in 1940 and was caught in the St. Valentine Day's blizzard). Along the old Carpenter path, he showed me where Ellery L. Goff had once run his steam powered portable shingle mill. The only sign of his past activity is a circle of blackened soil where the brush does not grow well. Our trip ended at the Bellanger lot on the shore of the swamp, the same lot where Roy and brother Elwood were cutting pines during the Valentine Day blizzard. Since then, the pines have thrived and are reaching such a size that I am sure Roy, if he were living, would be itching to convert them into pine lumber. Other than on that visit, all discoveries were made by me.

Once, while exploring at the Marvel Landing on the north end of the swamp, I found the ruins of a small stone foundation of a cabin. Nearby were the usual remnants—a bed spring and rusted out ironware. Travelling up the cart path toward Winthrop Street, I found another similar ruin of a habitation. Not far away stood the remains of a larger stone foundation that could have been used as a horse stable. I wondered who built, lived, and used these structures; what experiences and difficulties did they encounter in the Squannakonk Swamp? These questions will never be answered.

I had heard of Fuller's Island and Chestnut Island in the Swamp. From deeds and with Roy's directions, I was with some difficulty able to locate Fuller's Island. After some searching and sliding on the ice through thick brush and large trees, I finally found it a few hundred feet off the shore from the Maple Lane area. The Island is surrounded on three sides by fairly deep swamp, with water on the south side so shallow as to make it more a peninsula than an island. Roy told me that when he was a boy there was a path that ran westerly off Maple Lane into the swamp and over to Fuller's Island, across the Island, and southerly over land now owned by Winsor Tripp, and out to County Street. Roy recalled once accompanying his father on a sled pulled by a yoke of oxen on the path that crosses what is now the Tripp farm near County Street. The owner of the farm came out and from a distance ordered them off the property. Roy said his father just calmly kept the rig heading for the swamp, knowing that this was a legal way into the lower section of the Squannakonk Swamp. Roy's grandfather and father had used it along with other farmers for generations. Nothing further was said to the Hortons by the farm owners. Hardly a trace of this route can now be seen on the ground except the portion running from the end of Maple Lane to the swamp.

Years ago when exploring Fuller's Island, I unexpectedly happened upon a moss covered cord of wood carefully stacked on a spit of dry land on the shore; it was so old that the logs crumbled at the touch. I wondered who the woodcutter was that labored there long ago to cut and carefully stack his wood but never returned to remove it. Maybe he had been caught in a sudden thaw that made the swamp impassable; perhaps discouraged with this unexpected turn of events, he decided Squannakonk Swamp was a place to keep away from and never returned.

The location of Chestnut Island remained elusive to me for many years. I do not recall Roy ever mentioning it, but from old deed references I knew the Island existed somewhere in the Swamp. It was not until a couple of years ago while surveying that I found it was on the extreme end of the swamp and that one corner was crossed by County Street. Not knowing it, I had been driving over a portion of the Island for years.

One object that I have been unable to find despite a diligent search that even involved using surveying instruments is the Long Stone situated deep in the northern portion of the swamp. Many ancient deeds make mention of a long or tall stone set as a boundary marker. Since stones in this part of the swamp are a rarity, particularly a stone of that description, I am sure this marker was hauled in on a sled and set up in the swamp by a farmer 200 years or more ago. Since I had no trouble finding other stones only 12 inches tall in the easterly section of the swamp, I anticipated no trouble in locating a tall one. My search however was to no avail; possibly the stone fell over and is now buried in the muck.

Although very little cordwood has been cut in Squannakonk Swamp since the early 1920's, white pine and white cedar were still harvested at various times and places up into the late 1950's by Elwood and Roy Horton. At that time Elwood and his son Lyman cut cedar south of Vickery Point to use as top rails on their cow pasture walls. Cedar stumps from this work can still be seen. About the same time Roy and his nephew Frank

Coughlan and his son-in-law Francis McClellan cut some pine and cedar north of Maple Lane near the Bellanger Lot. The last horse that Roy owned, "Old Bill Horse," was used to sled the logs to the landing. Francis, who had never before done that type of work with a horse, recalls that Roy had had caulked shoes put on the horse by a blacksmith to prevent him from slipping on the ice. Even so, the horse was cautious when walking on the ice and even more so when he approached a soft wet unfrozen spot at the edge of the ice. As he approached the soft ground, he would carefully test it with one foot before putting his whole weight on it. Francis thought he must have had some bad memories of having once gotten mired down in a soft spot.

At present about 300 acres, nearly one half of Squannakonk Swamp, are owned by the author and his son, E. Otis Dyer, Jr. This area includes the William Marvel Swamp, Henry W. Horton Swamp, Charles Smith Swamp, and Ministerial Swamp. Other large swamp owners today are Richard and Helen L. Dennen, who own the same swamp that was once owned by Francis J. Wheeler at New Street, and the descendants of Christopher Carpenter (1762-1840), one of Rehoboth's earliest settlers to purchase land in the main part of Squannakonk Swamp and Little Squannakonk Swamp. One of Christopher's more famous descendants was Sinclair Weeks, the Secretary of the Interior for President Eisenhower.

The trees growing in Manwhague Swamp are of the same variety as those found in Squannakonk Swamp, but generally they are smaller. This is especially true at the north end where wood cutting activities tookplace at a later date than at Squannakonk Swamp. The last person to cut pine timber here was George Reed of Reed Brothers Farm on Williams Street, Dighton. Mr. Reed cut large quantities of pine in 1936 and had it hauled out over the Lindley Path and on to the Jillson sawmill which was still being operated by water power on the Segregansett River next to the Reed farm. Ernest (Moe) Horton over the years has cut firewood extensively along the border and into the northerly end of the swamp. John (Rabbitt) Rego (1912-1989) during the 1930's cut cordwood for the Cardoza family at the south end of the swamp near Log Neck. While cutting, like many before him, he had his razor sharp ax slip and slice through his boot into his foot. John had to hobble about one mile to his home with his boot full of blood to get medical aid.

The five approaches to Manwhague Swamp are still very discernible on the ground and portions of them are passable by truck or tractor. The two paths Roy used most often, the Stony Path leading southerly in from Cedar Street and the Lindley Path leading in easterly from Plain Street, are still very well defined on the ground. Some of these are still used by Moe Horton for access to his hay fields and to haul wood. The path or lane leading westerly into the swamp from Hornbine Road, the same path that Henry W. Horton used when he bought spiles from Emeline Chace in 1911 can still be followed into the swamp, although some parts have grown up somewhat in brush. Everett Gonsalves uses part of the lane for his driveway. The Log Neck Path is now part of the road into Rehoboth's Sanitary Land Fill. The remainder of the path is still easy to follow with the old wagon ruts being very noticeable on the ground. The path to the Rail Place on the west side of the swamp is on Nathalie Merchant's property. The path fades out near the shore of the swamp where the cedars were once hauled to the shore and split into rails before the days of barbed wire.

Today, Moe Horton has the best knowledge of the location of the swamp lot boundaries and lot owners. He has spent much of his life farming on the shores of the swamp and cutting wood and timber in the swamp. For generations he and his family have run a dairy farm on the border of Manwhague Swamp at 75 Plain Street, appropriately called Manwhague Farm. The Hortons' English style dairy barn that was built by Moe's father in 1910 from timber cut in Manwhague Swamp still stands. White pine was cut and sledded from the swamp to be used for the framing, siding, and roofing for the barn. White cedar was also cut and hauled to the water powered saw, grist, and shingle mill at the Perryville section of Rehoboth, where it was sawn into shingles for use on the barn roof and walls. Moe recalls that the shingles on the roof lasted 35 years, and the unpainted shingles used on the northerly walls where they were protected from the sun are still in fair condition today, over 80 years later.

Because of the numerous land divisions that have taken place in Manwhague Swamp over the years, the original lot layout has become more fragmented than the layout in

Squannakonk Swamp, especially in the middle section of the Manwhague Swamp where the 160 Rod and 92 Rod Swamps are located. The largest owner of the Manwhague Swamp lots today is the Rehoboth Conservation Commission which owns the Joseph Lunan and Sons land, the same people who in 1910 built a crude railroad into the swamp to harvest the pine and cedar.

Moe Horton standing in front of his barn on his Manwhague Farm, Plain Street, Rehoboth. The timbers and shingles for the barn were cut in Manwhague Swamp about 1910 and sawn into lumber at the Perryville Mill, Rehoboth.

The Horton Farm House
"Manwhague" Plain Street, Rehoboth

Chapter III

GREAT MEADOW HILL TODAY

Although Great Meadow Hill has seen much more change than have the swamps of easterly Rehoboth, in general, since Sam Smith and his sons ceased wood cutting activities on the Hill 50 or 60 years ago, there has been little development in comparison with other parts of Rehoboth. During this interval, the undisturbed oak and beech trees have in many places had time to reach maturity. The greatest change to the Hill however, occurred in 1955 when the United States Government found that its high elevation would make a suitable site for the radar portion of a Nike - Hercules anti-aircraft missile battery. The Cold War was being raged with Russia and it was feared that Russian bombers would attack Providence. A series of hills was selected on a 10 mile radius around that city for the installation of these missiles and Great Meadow Hill was chosen for one of them. To make room for the new radar equipment and its associated troop quarters, the government's contractors began to level off the top of the hill. The missiles themselves and associated facilities were installed about one mile east of the radar site on Buck's Hill where the Rehoboth town offices are now located. This anti-aircraft system became obsolete by the early 1960's when the long range ballistic missile replaced aircraft as a main offensive weapon.

About 20 years ago, the missile facility was declared surplus by the Federal Government and given to the Town of Rehoboth. It is now used for municipal offices and a Town dog pound. The site on Great Meadow Hill is still a military installation and is presently the headquarters of the 26th Infantry Division Artillery of the Massachusetts National Guard. As mentioned before, Great Meadow Hill has had previous military significance when in 1778 the Rehoboth militia chose to use its high elevation to erect a signal beacon to warn Minute Men toward the north of the beginning of a British raid towards Providence from Newport. The beacon stood a few hundred feet north of the radar installation. Again 177 years later, the Hill was still being used to protect Providence but this time against a different enemy, a case of history repeating itself.

Since a large amount of soil, gravel, and rocks were declared surplus when the top of the Hill was leveled to accommodate the new buildings for the Nike site, large quantities of these materials were trucked to the foot of the Hill to fill in swampy areas. This move occurred decades before the passage of the wet land protection laws in force today. For access to the Nike-Hercules radar installation, the government's contractors built a modern paved road to the site from dusty gravely Fairview Avenue. The new road followed the ancient cart path that had run up over the Hill just west of the fire tower. This was the main path that wood operators like Sam Smith, David W. Francis and George L. Goff, had used to haul out their cordwood cut from the top and the north slope of the Hill.

Before the top of the Hill was regraded, the fire tower was dismantled and moved to a new site on Long Hill on Reservoir Avenue, but at a lower elevation, where it is still situated today. Since Great Meadow Hill is considerably higher than the new location, the fire spotter in the tower sometimes has had trouble locating fires beyond the Hill. Although the fire tower has been gone from Great Meadow Hill for almost 40 years and its former site completely obliterated, its location was memorialized when the local people named the Nike site's new access road Fire Tower Road. Once I found an interesting artifact that was formerly associated with the tower. While walking down the west slope of the Hill, I noticed a glass insulator fastened on a short twisted wire hanging on an old gnarled black oak. I recognized it as an insulator used to support the iron telephone wire when it ran through the forest from the tower to Fairview Avenue. To connect a phone in the tower to the new telephone exchange near Rehoboth Village, a line had been strung out to Fairview Avenue and on to Anawan Street. What seems strange now was that the line was run across private property in the most direct line through the woods down the west slope of the

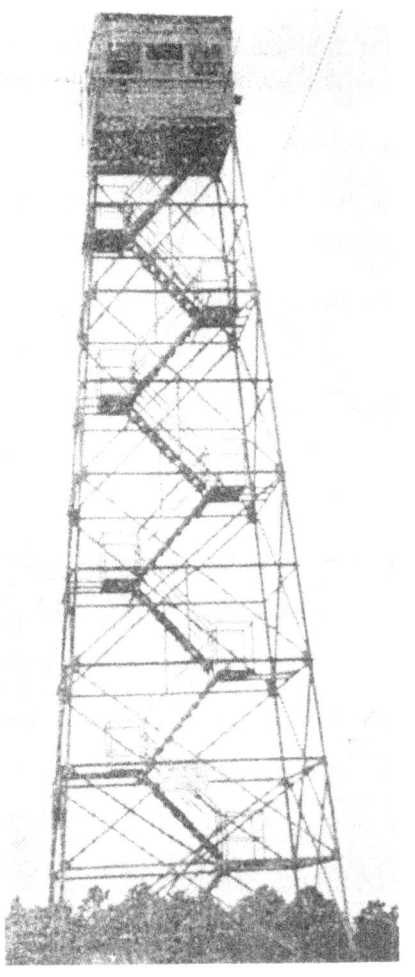

Jun 15, 1955
STEPPING ASIDE FOR PROGRESS — A last look at the forest fire observation tower atop Great Meadow Hill in Rehoboth, is provided in this photo before razing operations start to make room for a Nike guided missile site. The Rehoboth tower landmark has been at its present location since 1915.

Taunton Gazette
Photo and Caption

Same view today

Hill and across the farm now owned by the author, rather than being installed along a road where maintenance would have been much easier. Chestnut trees growing on the hill were cut and used for poles where needed, but whenever possible, the heavy iron wire was attached to large oak trees with insulators, one of which I had found. Until about 25 years ago a few of the original chestnut telephone poles that were used in the open land on the Great Meadow Hill Farm at the foot of the Hill were still standing, witness to the durability of the chestnut tree as a post without the application of any wood preservative.

Taking advantage of the newly paved Fire Tower Road, developers have built several new houses along the road over the years, giving that side of the Hill a little more suburban look. Except for these changes and a series of houses built on large lots running up the easterly slope of the Hill on Francis Street after that street was paved during the 1960's, very few other improvements have taken place there.

Exploring Great Meadow Hill to discover signs of previous uses and occupation has been, like investigating the Rehoboth swamps, a favorite pastime of mine. The paths used by Smith, Francis, and Goff, and other wood operators from the earliest days of the settlement of Rehoboth are still distinguishable on the ground. The old bridge site across the East Branch of the Palmer River can still be seen, but the bridge where Sam Smith as a boy saw a string of horses pulling a loaded wagon across has long rotted away. Downstream the bridge on the path from the Hill to Billings Road also has long ago decayed away and been replaced in 1985 by a more permanent structure. Beside it, the old fording place used by wagons when the bridge was out is still being used by horseback riders. Some of the cart paths have grown up with brush, while others like the last mentioned bridge have been improved upon to allow the passage of farm machinery used on the Great Meadow Hill Farm. The apple orchard and sheep pen located in the early 1800's on the western terrace of the Hill are now a corn and hay field connected with that Farm.

Once, while walking on the path that runs along the terrace from that field toward Fairview Avenue, I noticed a large smooth rock beside an old wheel rut. This stone had a peculiar

"L" shaped notch on its side toward the path that did not seem natural. Upon closer examination I could see that it was manmade, but at first I could not think of its purpose or who would have taken the time to chisel it out. Then I realized it had been ground to that shape by countless wagons loaded with wood rolling along the path to the stacking area on Fairview Avenue. The stone was in such a position that the iron tires on the left wheels of the wagon would strike the stone, ride up on it, and then slide down its face, each time scraping off a little stone dust. I paused a moment trying to visualize the number of wagons that had to have passed over that path over the years in order to cut out that groove; there had to have been thousands.

Even though 150 years have passed, if one looks carefully on the top of the Hill just north of the Nike site, signs can still be discerned that sum up the whole history of the land use on the Hill from the days the Davis family planted the top of the Hill with corn to the days when the land was reclaimed by the forest. Not far from where the beacon from Revolutionary War days stood stands an ancient gnarled white oak. The tree stands out sharply from the much younger forest around it. Despite its age, the tree is not as tall as its neighbors; its branches are large and close to the ground and extend out perpendicular from the old trunk in contrast to the lack of lower branches and the high crowns of the surrounding forest. Obviously, when this tree was young, there being no forest here, it was able to leisurely throw out its branches and did not have to exert energy in gaining height quickly to avoid being blocked from the sun by its neighbors. It actually resembles an old shade tree growing in someone's yard rather than a forest tree. A tree of this type is called a "pasture oak" or "cow tree", meaning that as cultivated land was allowed to turn into pasture, a good solid tree was often allowed to grow to provide shade for the cows to gather about on a hot day to rest. This tree has stood witness to a series of land changes on the hill from tillage to pasture to mature woodland.

Just north of the cow tree there is evidence of use of this land after it had reverted back to forest. One day while walking near the cow tree I noticed a slight but rectangular depression in the ground barely noticeable under a cover of new leaves and leaf mould. Since it did not look as though it was a natural feature, I began scrapping away some of the top soil and debris. Finding blackened soil covered with little pieces of charcoal, I realized I had discovered the site of one of the old charcoal burning pits. Since the land here once belonged to George Hathaway Goff, the wood operator from New Street, no doubt this was probably one of his or his son Arthur Goff's charcoal pits.

As in the swamps, the wood lots on Great Meadow Hill have been named after nineteenth century owners with the exception of the Davis-Smith Hill Top Field on top of the Hill and the Big Back Pasture at the foot of the east slope of the Hill on the former Sam Smith farm. Most of the lots are fairly regular in shape and range in size from a few acres to 10 or 15 acres. On the lower west slope of the Hill is the Edmond Peck Lot. Just up the Hill above it is the Elnathan Jones lot; higher up over that is the woodlot with the unusual name of Vashty Bowen Penno. The first two of these lots were acquired by my family in 1822 and 1837 respectively and, in the usual manner, named after the seller. The latter lot was originally bought from Edmund Peck in 1823 and passed into the hands of a daughter Vashty Bowen (1800-1868). Vashty later married a Penno and those names have been associated with that lot ever since. Vashty lived out her final years in a little cottage off Pond Lily Avenue not far away. Other lots on the west side of the hill were named after Hezekiah Short who lived at what is now 83 Peck Street, John Davis II who lived at what is now 225 Anawan Street, Ruth Waterman who once lived on Anawan Street, Enos Round who lived at what is now 180 Anawan Street, and Stephen Carpenter who lived at what is now 23 Bay State Road.

The Commonwealth of Massachusetts took an interest in some of these lots during the depression of the 1930's. Their value had fallen very low and they were barely worth the wood standing on them. The State began a program by which these low value lots could be voluntarily sold to the State. Even though the price paid was only a few dollars an acre, some owners decided selling was better than receiving nothing and losing the land for nonpayment of taxes. Sam Smith, the Short family, and Maxim Salvas were quick to take advantage of this program by cutting the wood off their lots and then selling them to the State. Everett Short of Peck Street sold to the State a large portion of his farm on Francis Street and Peck Street. Sales by Sam Smith included the Enos Rounds Lot and other lots, but the wood on the Vashty Bowen Penno Lot was still in the process of being cut off in preparation to selling to the State when the program was abandoned.

Another purpose the State had for acquiring these parcels, other than to alleviate the tax burden on the owners, was to build a ski slope. Both the very steep west and east slopes of the Hill would have provided a fast run for a skier, and the north slope with its much easier gradient would have been more suitable for a novice. When these plans became known, there was considerable excitement in the neighborhood from people thinking of ways to cash in on the ski crowd that would soon be appearing. The area was very depressed at the time and the people were living at the poverty level; in their houses water was still being pumped by hand and kerosene was used for lighting. A ski resort would have been a bonanza to the neighborhood. Unfortunately for the residents, the plan was soon dropped and the land that had been purchased by the State is now what is known as the Rehoboth State Forest.

In 1975 admirers of H. P. Lovecraft (1890-1936), having studied his letters and having noted his references to his Great Meadow Country Club, became curious about what remains of it might be found today. One day they visited with me at the site of the old club house. From 1946 until recently, the property on which it had stood was owned by Henry and Flossie Flibotte. The Flibottes at the time built a small house on the west side of the cart path by the fire tower which later was to become the Fire Tower Road. A little south of their new house stood an old stone fireplace. The Flibottes had not the slightest idea who built it or that it was connected with a famous literary figure. Over the years the Flibotte family occasionally used the fireplace for family cookouts. When the Lovecraft enthusiasts and I discovered the initials G.M.C.C. (Great Meadow Country Club) set in the cement hearth of the fireplace, we knew we had found the site of the Lovecraft cabin. Lovecraft had written that those initials had been set by him in the wet cement when the hearth was being built. H. P. Lovecraft wrote a letter about this last visit to the club house which is considered by some a classic eulogy to lost youth. A portion of his letter is as follows:

> Our youth came again upon us like a flame. For there amidst the growing trees in awkward grace stood the symbol of our old days in wonted wholeness — the boyhood clubhouse erect in its tar-papered grotesqueness, and intact in every part through all the years!! There was neither vandalism nor decay - the lock was gone, but that was all. Even the old pictures hung on the walls of this haunted place; this little world of the past, where even time has eased his scourging in the absence of any human audience. What shadowy companies, moreover, could we picture about the grey cement hearth where the pebbled initials G. M. C. C. still lay fixed as we had stamped them when it was new and wet! We seemed to see the old gang as it was- Ron, and Ken, and Stuart, with the fresh faces and clear eyes of youth. They are not dead, but the boy in them is dead, so that their ghosts appear only in this silent and forgotten place. And as we gazed about, Harold conceived the idea of regaining for brief snatches the youth that we had lost. If all goes well, we shall refit this house of miraculous preservation and bring back to it the men who were once the old gang and perhaps on some nights in the golden autumn when the logs burn red in the stone fireplace the ghosts may pass back into the aging bodies to which they belonged of old, and the gang will lie once again. And perhaps we shall sing in the olden way, and teach the birds of autumn the songs known to the birds of other autumns, and awake the old trees to memories of strains that stirred leaves now fallen...

Mr. Lovecraft died in 1936 at age 46. The stone fireplace still stands a short distance to the west of Fire Tower Road.

E. Otis Dyer at the H. P. Lovecraft fireplace at the site of the Great Meadow Country Club Cabin on Fire Tower Road.

LOST ON GREAT MEADOW HILL

On July 23rd Maria and I
went picking blueberries way up high,
High in the lots of Great Meadow Hill
with two wooden pails we intended to fill.
We began at eleven with our picnic lunch;
egg salad sandwiches, cold sassafras punch.
The picking was best along the edge
where high bush blueberries formed a hedge
with sumac, poison ivy, and thorn
around John Davis' field of corn.
When the sun was low and red in the sky,
out of the shadows came a hoard of deer flies.
Far below were our house and barn and shed,
and the cows walking home, so Maria said,
"straight down the hill," we could get home quick
and maybe find more blueberries to pick.
There's a path through the Vashty Bowen Penno Lot, I know;
that's how we'll get home to our farm below.
We could see the direction from where we stood

so we descended through bull briars into the wood.
Down across ledges of pudding stone
through the secretive aspens to Elnathan Jones.
Then through ferns on mossy damp ground
down into the gloom of Enos Rounds.
It was at this point that Maria guessed
incorrectly that we were heading west,
back to our supper and feather beds
to our chores in the kitchen and milking shed.
The moss grew thick on the bark all around.
There were no clues left on the level ground.
Then the sun was gone quite suddenly,
and the grinning moon climbed through the trees.
It did us no good to shout and call,
no one called back or came at all.
Our bed of leaf mould was rather damp,
but we didn't sleep much in that little camp.
Instead we told stories in brave cheerful voices
recited poems, sang hymns, and then listened to noises.
We found it most useful to list and discuss
exactly which animals might be lurking near us.
After all it's Rehoboth; our minds set at ease,
no boa constrictors would drop from the trees.
Just at dawn we heard shouts to which we replied,
soon our brother Enoch was at our side,
And how quickly we saw where we'd spent the night,
the obvious land marks revealed in the light.
Here were the red cedar trees standing tall
in the Edmund Peck lot enclosed by a wall.
So we told for the first time, by no means the last
how our night on Great Meadow Hill had passed.
But would we have guessed after decades of time
that our tale would be told in couplets and rhyme?

by Betsey Dexter Dyer

Based on a family tradition in the author's family that his great-grandmother Maria Bowen Dexter (1840-1936) and her sister Harriet A. Bowen Peck (1842-1932) were lost overnight on the Hill blueberrying circa 1855.

Chapter IV

ROY W. HORTON, SWAMP YANKEE

It was always pleasant for me to visit with Roy. Our conversations were invariably interesting and informative. Roy liked people and enjoyed discussing personalities he had met over the years, usually in connection with his farm or carpentry business. Those conversations were not gossipy in nature but rather about experiences with people he had known and their family relationships. Sometimes he enjoyed just trying to figure out why some people acted the way they did and how to best relate his personality to theirs.

Not long after I first met him, Roy and his wife Elsie moved to a new house they had built on Horton Street in Dighton, a little north of the old Elder Goff Meeting House on a portion of the farm once owned by his grandfather James H. Horton. The house was a full 1 1/2 story cape, Roy's favorite house style, which he and Elsie had designed just for their needs. One of its main features was a comfortable den built into the cellar for Roy's use. By building the house into the side of a hill, Roy had created a cellar room with a large sunny window and a walk-in ground level entrance door. Roy spent much of his time in his den when at home, particularly later in life after he had become almost totally crippled with knee problems. The first and second floors of the home were attractively furnished and meticulously maintained by Elsie, but Roy always seemed a little uncomfortable in these surroundings and preferred relaxing in his den.

The den was built of materials and furnished with items that were typically Roy. The walls were sheathed with native white pine boards sawed from trees that he had cut himself from the Bellanger and Abigail Moulton lots in Squannakonk Swamp. In one corner was a cot for an afternoon nap; beside that was a bookcase full of books on historical and farm subjects. On the walls were pictures of people and past activities that had meant much to Roy: a picture of his oldest brother Harlan who had died young and of his father as a younger man standing beside a yoke of oxen. Over in the corner were a few comfortable chairs circling a wood stove which during the winter months often had a crackling fire in it. In the unfinished part of the cellar there was a small work shop where he kept his carpentry tools and a row of stove wood carefully stacked against one wall. A special cellar entrance had been built near the driveway so Roy's visitors could enter the den from the outside without traipsing through the upstairs rooms with muddy boots.

Often when I had encountered a problem in my surveying work that involved locating members of old Dighton families, I found Roy's knowledge of family relationships impressive. Not only did he know where the children and grandchildren in question presently lived and how they were related, but he would also recall some interesting fact about their personalities and perhaps give an anecdote about an experience he had with them. From there, one thing usually led to another and sometimes, before I knew it, a couple of hours had passed, particularly if we were sitting around the fire on a cold winter's day. Roy always conversed in an easy quiet manner and never tried to dominate the conversation. He was always just as interested in my viewpoint as in expressing his own.

Roy was a keen observer of the business world and always had words of advice for me: "Keep the size of your business small and manageable. Sometimes there is a tendency to expand too fast in good economic times, but you will only regret it later when you find yourself over extended when the economy slows." He was a firm believer in Benjamin Franklin's old adage, "If you don't run your business, your business will run you." As an example he would often cite situations in which a carpenter he knew was successful at first and then would begin to expand his business rapidly, often too rapidly, and end up in bankruptcy when the real estate market collapsed. There was one young builder in the area well known to the Horton family who had expanded his business quickly. Some of Roy's friends, noticing this builder's success in constructing several houses on speculation at the same time, asked Roy why he didn't do the same. Roy's reply was one of his favorite comments which I think he learned from his father, "We shall see." Sure enough, the real estate market fell, the man was unable to sell the houses he had built, and he was forced into bankruptcy. Roy's policy was to build one house at a time, preferably for the owner. If he ever did build a speculation house, he sold it before beginning another. Also, many builders as their business expanded would build an office, small warehouse, and storage yard for their materials. Roy considered these unnecessary expenses and instead operated his carpentry business from the dining room table in his house. From here he did all his own bookkeeping, payroll, and job estimating work. For his warehouse he used his grandfather's old cow barn on Wellington Street.

Roy was never really interested in making a lot of money, even though that impression may have been given when he began to talk about wood operators. If the firewood market had still existed, there is no doubt Roy would have liked to have "cleaned up" in it. I am sure that, like David W. Francis, he would have taken advantage of every opportunity to make a large profit, just as Roy and his father never ceased trying "to make a killing" in the late tomato wholesale market in Providence. Even though these terms, *making a killing* and *cleaning up,* were two of Roy's favorites when talking about farm market opportunities, making money for money's sake was not what chiefly motivated Roy and his father. Both men wanted to make enough money to support themselves and their families comfortably and to give themselves the economic freedom to do some of the things that were enjoyable to them, but not to earn money necessarily for high profits; they enjoyed raising a yoke of oxen for the fun of it or buying a Jersey heifer for a grandson and helping him raise it. Even though Roy never stopped trying "to make a killing" on late tomatoes until he was no longer able, I never heard a complaint from him when his crop failed or when the market, beginning to show promise, suddenly would collapse from the late tomatoes trucked in from New Jersey and the southern states. It was not so much making the money that was important to Roy, but the challenge of attempting an enterprise and seeing it succeed.

Roy also had other advice for me. When we discussed how

best to solve a business disagreement that sometimes occurs with a client, he would advise me that the best tactic is not to become argumentative if the client begins to become abusive, as sometimes happens, but to say in a calm manner, "Now we have a problem. There is disagreement, and now what are we going to do about it?" Usually, Roy would say, such an approach has a calming effect and soon some agreeable compromise would occur so that perhaps you might still end up as friends. That has not always been easy advice to follow, but I found that it sometimes does work.

I recall that once Roy used a variation of that calming tactic on me. When we had a difference of opinion on how to construct a logging sled that we were working on, he did not press his idea on me but left me to proceed on my own. An argument was avoided because there was no one to argue with, and after further thought I soon realized he was right and we proceeded to finish the work together. The difference had come about when I expressed an interest in owning a logging sled of the type Roy used to build. Without hesitation he said he would help me build the sled if I could get the material together. First he told me to cut down a large white oak tree and have it sawn at a sawmill into two heavy planks 3 inches by 16 inches by 10 feet and into a few 2 inch by 10 inch planks. When I called him to say these were ready, he told me to meet him at his former grandfather's house on Wellington Street to scavenge the pieces of iron from some of his old logging sleds to use on the new sled. We found what we wanted at the Birch Hill lot, the apparent graveyard for the Hortons' abandoned sleds. After picking up the iron needed, we went further into the lot and cut a suitable hickory tree about four or five inches in diameter for the taps.

Once all the materials had been gathered, Roy appeared one day at my farm to begin the work of assembling the sled. Since it was a cold winter's day, I cleared up a place inside my work shed, started a fire in the stove, and laid out the materials. A couple of my employees were there to help. Roy showed us how to cut out ellipses for the front of the runners out of the two large planks. Roy had brought along a special type of drill from the nineteenth century that I had never seen before; it was old enough to have belonged to his grandfather. It was

E. Otis Dyer stands beside the type of logging sled used at the Horton farm, built under the direction of Roy W. Horton.

The runner taps have been changed from wood to steel on this sled.

rather a large rectangular contraption made of wood and iron, similar to a large egg beater. The drill bit was turned by a hand crank arrangement that rotated the bit through a gear reduction drive. It was slow but powerful and it proved to be an effective way of drilling through the heavy green wood. After the holes were drilled, the sled was bolted together with an angle iron and large bolts.

Now came the difficult part of putting the taps on the bottom of the runners. Taps protected the main frame of the sled from wear and were replaceable. To make the taps, the hickory tree we had cut was split into two equal sections lengthwise. One end of the tap was inserted into an iron stirrup that had been bolted to the front of the sled runner. Roy took over the delicate yet strenuous task of bending the tap around the elliptical section of the runner. The tap was green, tough, and resilient and did not bend easily. Roy's method, the one that the Hortons had developed over the years, was to have one person put his weight on the tap and another person hold what had been gained by wrapping a chain around the sled runner and tap. Little by little as the tap was bent down the chain was tightened. Becoming impatient with what seemed to be a slow process, I suggested to Roy that we set my hydraulic jack on top of the tap and with a 2 by 4 wedged against the shed ceiling, jack the tap down into place. He gave me a smile, offered no opposition to the idea, and indicated to me to go ahead. Obviously he did not want anything to do with my plan and characteristically he did not begin to argue why his method was better as most persons would have done. His attitude was, "why argue, you will soon see for yourself that my method is right." I soon began to have misgivings about what I was trying to do and asked him why he did not like my idea. He said that if the jack slips off, the tap will fly up like a catapult and who knows what or whom it may hit. He recalled that once his brother Raymond was forcing a tap down into place when the chain holding it slipped off. As the tap sprang up, it took Raymond with it and threw him across the room. My jack idea for the sled was quickly dropped and under Roy's direction the work was safely completed.

Roy drew from his lifetime of experience to tell me that the worst characteristic he noticed in people was jealousy. He had seen some families torn apart by it. He noted that, when a brother or a sister thinks the parents are giving more favors or some additional economic help to one of the siblings or when one member of the family seems to be doing better or getting ahead faster that another, there is often jealousy. In his own family, Roy could recall one member making some snide remarks about another member behind his back. Somehow word of that person's sarcasm got to the person being criticized and so, in turn, he retaliated with some cutting remarks of his own and so it went. However, Roy noticed that sometimes when you think brother hates brother, some emergency may come up or one of them may get into some difficulty, and then past differences are quickly forgotten and everyone does what he can to help. Roy said that among his own relatives and acquaintances he had seen that happen plenty of times.

Roy was known in the community for his honesty and integrity. In business dealings, when he said he would perform a task, whether it was to build a small shed or a whole house, his word could be counted on. Many people, including me, had houses or additions built by Roy with a business contract of no more than a hand shake; seldom was anything ever put in writing. Once Roy figured out the work and material needed, he could be counted on to perform the work as shown on the plans and for the price agreed upon. Later in life after he had retired from active carpentering he was much sought after to "housesit" for people when they were away vacationing. Without reservation, the keys of the house would be entrusted to Roy so that each day he could inspect the property inside as well as out.

When World War II began, Roy was hired at 75 cents per hour by a contractor to do carpentry work on the army barracks being built at Camp Edwards on Cape Cod and later at Camp Myles Standish in Taunton and in the Hingham Shipyard. Roy never got over his astonishment from once watching a carpenter working beside him on a roof or wall, putting in only one nail at a joint or none at all, while Roy was conscientiously putting in the required three nails. When Roy asked his partner why he was not properly fastening the boards, the reply was, "What do you care, the government is paying for it." Roy with his upbringing could not believe that there were actually people who would do that shoddy type of work.

Roy's love of nature led him during the latter years of his life to become one of the chief supporters of a wild life sanctuary in West Dighton. A friend of his, D. Lee Johnson, had founded the Southern New England Bird Watchers and was looking for an area to establish a bird sanctuary. Roy was called upon to help and generously he offered for a site the use of land he owned, "over at Shubes," off the end of Winfield Lane. The land offered was the ten acre Thomas Witherell Lot once owned by Roy's father and part of the purchase made by the Hortons in 1919 from David W. Francis. Volunteers cleared away the underbrush in a wooded area and built a rustic platform on which they held outdoor lectures on nature; nature walks were laid out and during the winter feeding stations for the birds were established.* The sanctuary was named the Horton Memorial Wildlife Sanctuary to honor a long history of community service and love of nature on the part of the Horton family, a particularly fitting tribute to Roy Horton, the quintessential swamp yankee and to his lifetime consonant with the natural rhythms of field and swamp.

* The sanctuary was operated successfully for several years and finally closed when Roy became too infirm to help care for it. The land is still in its natural state and owned by Roy's daughter Janice.

APPENDIX I

ROY W. HORTON
UNCLE ROY, "JOE"
BY
FRANK COUGHLAN

Eulogy given at the memorial service of Roy Horton
January 8, 1989

I'll start my story of my life with Roy with a story Roy told me of his early days. It was that of being a young boy, 12 or 13 -ish, and of his father having Roy drive a horse team and wagon to Providence, to market. Of a young boy finding a spot to park the wagon at the loading platform in the early morning darkness and doing the paperwork with the Produce Dealers there. Perhaps on the way home, stopping at the *Black-Smith's Shop* or the *Hardware Store* to pick up a repaired harness or some hardware items. Many times parts of this story of these trips to market were told to me, riding wagon in the cold or bad weather, the dark early morn, the horses knowing the way, the time involved to make these trips, the fact that Dad trusted young Roy to do the duty, the fact that his Dad could do important work at the barn. I felt in a way that "I" had been able to make some of these journeys with Roy. The stories showed the deep respect Roy had for his father, good with men, good as a businessman, good family man, good with animals, horses and cattle, good with produce and timber. Good manager of the things of the rural community.

I think this started Roy along the road of providing himself with jobs, in lean years, when it took a scratching out of odd jobs, to dig here and there to make a living. With his on the farm training for the work world of his day. There was the entering into the carpentering trade with its discipline and apprenticeship. Then striking out on his own, he and Tink. That's where the name "Joe" came from, Roy and Percy called each other names.

Oh yes, the stories of school day pranks "cutting up country style." Remember the long string, stretched over the house blind and rubbing on the string made that groaning sound in the house and the old man (by Fish School) would run out and chase them. And hoeing in the fields all day with "Old John" a faithful farm helper that young Roy worked with. And working the horse and tip cart, shoveling gravel all day - his father provided gravel for the town roads. And Camp Edwards during the war years. And Model A Ford stories. Building houses (cottages) at Little Compton, R.I. - many houses in this town are Roy W. Horton.

I've tried to set a scene of a young farm boy Roy, in the horse and wagon days, with some teams of oxen in there too, thru the young man's apprentice days of learning a trade and striking out on his own, of lean times and of young married life down the lane at "Shubael's" with that pretty Evans girl from the city.

Well Roy's wife had sisters and well that makes cousins - I want to tell you, they are some of the best. And as a young boy, I spent time on the farm (not all city kids can do that). But young "Frankie" went into the poultry houses with cousins to gather the eggs, or pluck off the feathers or climb on roofs. Yes, there were times Frank had to be cared for and he lived on Roy's farm, and cousins and Aunt Elsie washed and fed me. And I came to have chores of my own. Feed the chickens and sheep and then cattle, a little older now, and able to shovel out under the barn and drive tractor and spread on the fields. And what kid of the "50'as" got to haul water to the oxen and yoke them up. "Haw and Gee and Whoa, long after they stop." Salt and pepper were some of the Horton oxen.

You see Roy had it in him, from his Dad, to give a young boy jobs to do. No. I didn't take a team to Providence, but I did have corn to weed and cultivate, with Planet Junior garden tractor, and yes, more teams; Remember Wilma, Betty - Fred and Barney, Devon cattle, that paraded in the Taunton Bi-Centennial - son-in-law Frannie got to lead them in that outing, Roys' knees were not so good - he road the float.

But I had to strike out on my own, and from weekend part time, to learning and then working the same trade, I got to work with "Joe". Fix a sill in this old building, crawl under Francis Farm and fix the floor, or put shingles on the roof. Drive to Grossman, spend all day sorting out the best boards - sight down 'em - crowns all this way - "that a boy." Cold weather - in the woods, axe and two man saw, he's 50+ and I'm 20'as trying to keep up to Joe. Cut cedar posts and bring 'em out, let's see, make some 40 ft. trusses, they are going for the exhibit building at the Rehoboth Fair, one building has his name on it now. Oh yeah, it's Thursday night the green Ford pickup is there, yes Roy's the judge of the ox pulling. Yes Roy starts the engine now and then to warm up the cab and that's Mr. Tripp sitting there again.

Yes I think by now you can see the deep respect and love I have of this man, who in many ways was as a father to me.

The story shows him to be good with men, good as a businessman, good family man, good with animals and building materials - "good manager of the things of a rural community." Drive down the street behind his pickup truck - oh well, none of us is perfect; remember, he is from the horse and wagon days.

But now I am middle age and on occasion Roy will want to feel my arm as his walker will assist him into church, just about every Sunday. Oh yes, my instruction included Roy's testimony and his example.

When it came time to re-open this church Roy and his brothers played a big part. And he could tell you of its helpers and its history.

Now see, he is very gentle and easy to care for in these days of older age. And for those knees, had to rebuild one of 'em twice. Good thing to have three daughters and a loving wife. The tides turned now, they care for his needs. And Elsie, up and down those stairs.

"Hello Pastor John" - nice of you to come to see me again - "your a good man", "yes I'm keeping short accounts."

YES YES, he says as he is cared for - no complaints from this man - but see - there is that conviction, that hope, that belief - that readiness. The time for "Joe" has come - thank you Lord, your will is done. We take comfort in the Lord. This is my story for "Joe".

APPENDIX II
The Meaning of the Term *Swamp Yankee*

The meaning of the term *Swamp Yankee* is controversial today. In 1989 Marion Harris of Morristown, New Jersey, had a conversation with me on this subject. In an informal telephone poll she had interviewed a number of Yankees living in towns along the Connecticut, Rhode Island, and Massachusetts coast and inland areas. People interviewed were asked if they had ever heard of the term *Swamp Yankee* and if so, did they consider it a compliment to be called by that name. By far she found that most people who knew the term found it complimentary. Also, from that poll she found that the term was generally known along the southeasterly coast of New England and that the older the person, the more likely he was to have heard of the term.

In an article in the *Providence Evening Bulletin* on December 16, 1983, columnist Mark Patinkin considered the meaning of the term. After some discussion, he concluded that a Swamp Yankee is "a rural, southern, New Englander, whose family dates to the Revolution; one who is frugal, not wealthy, laconic, not wordy, self reliant, earthy and proud."

An obituary in the *Providence Journal* on October 26, 1993, described how Samuel H. Cornell, age 92 of West Kingston, Rhode Island, as a 15 year boy drove an oxcart and sold firewood for a dollar a cord; later it described how he sold tractors, dug for quahogs, built skiffs, drove a taxi, constructed several buildings at Camp Hoffman Girl Scout Camp, and retired from the maintenance department of the University of Rhode Island. He was also a past president and organizer of Model A and antique auto clubs. He referred to himself as a true Swamp Yankee.

In the *Boston* magazine issue of September 1992, in an article called the "Tinkering Taylors", the family that owns the *Boston Globe*, a description was given how the founder of that paper, General Charles Taylor was known as a Swamp Yankee during his early years. As a young man, he was notable because whatever "he lacked in money and breeding he made up with pure amibition," a trait therewith associated with Swamp Yankeeism.

APPENDIX III
Additional Dairy Economics

Ernest L. Goff, Jr. (1907-   ) Broad Street Rehoboth, a retired dairy farmer, in an interview gave me further details of the milk economy during the first decades of this century.

Back in 1910 when Ernest's grandfather, William P. Gardiner, was running what was to become the Goff farm, the farmer was receiving about 5 to 5½¢ per quart and retailers usually doubled that price. After World War I there was a short lived bonanza for the farmer when the wholesale price of milk went to 10¢ per quart or $1.00 for a 10 quart can. Ernest noted that the cans the farmer used to ship milk to the dairy were originally 10 quart capacity; later they went to 20 quart size, and for many years until bulk tanks came in, 40 quart cans were used. Since 1 quart of milk weigh about 2.1 lbs. and the can itself weighs about 20 pounds, the new cans had a total weight of around 106 pounds and were very heavy to handle; many a farmer ended up with back problems from lifting these cans from the cooler into the truck.

When Ernest took over his grandfather's farm in 1932, his goal was to earn $24.00 gross per day. Since milk was then selling at 6¢ per quart, he planned to produce 400 quarts per day. For this amount, 30 to 33 milking cows were needed. In later years during the 1950's to make a decent living Ernest found he had to milk over twice that number of cows and needed two farms. While many farmers raised their own replacement cows by breeding their milk cows, Ernest found this practice unwise. He noted that a good dairy cow was difficult to breed and found it more profitable to buy his replacement cows. Every year he sold about one third of his milking cows and replaced them with new stock. Under this program the average life expectancy of a cow was about 5 to 6 years, though a well cared for cow kept to old age might live to age 15 or more.

APPENDIX IV

A list of farms and woodlots owned by Henry Wheaton Horton at the time of his death in 1943

DIGHTON

Home farm house, barn and various buildings, Wellington Street	35 acres
"Shubes" Farm, house and shed *	5 acres
Remainder of James H. Horton farm east side of Horton Street	43 acres
Tinkham Farm, Smith Street	35 acres
Nelson (Nate) Horton woodlot, Smith Street	9 acres
Lucinda (Lucindy) Horton woodlot, Smith Street	11 acres
Submit Briggs woodlot, Wellington Street	7 acres
Philip (Macker woodlot off Horton Street	3 acres
Kelton Swamp off Cedar Street (Manwhague Swamp)	16 acres
Nathan S. Earle woodlot	18 acres
F. J. Wheeler woodlot off Horton Street	4 acres
Thomas Witherell woodlot, Horton Street *	10 acres
Benjamin Goff off Oak Street *	8 acres
Andrew Goff woodlot off Horton Street *	8 acres
Emeline Goff woodlot off Horton Street *	2 acres
John Briggs woodlot	4 acres
Caleb Briggs woodlot	4 acres

REHOBOTH

The Earle woodlot off Reservoir Avenue	7 acres
Bellinger woodlot, Squannakonk Swamp	14 acres
Moulton woodlot, Simmons Street	12 acres
Mary Martin woodlot, Cedar Street	4 acres
Francis woodlot, Reservoir Avenue	5 acres
Amanda Brown Swamp Lot in Squannakonk Swamp	2 acres
The Viall Swamp Lot in Squannakonk Swamp	5 acres

Elbridge Martin Swamp Lot in Manwhague Swamp	6 acres
Lee Swamp Lot in Bad Luck Swamp	8 acres
Blanding Swamp Lot in Squannakonk Swamp	3 acres
Fred Goff woodlot off County Street	10 acres
TOTAL	298 acres

* Part of the old Elder Enoch Goff farm and David W. Francis purchase.

Source: Henry W. Horton Estate, Probate 80645

APPENDIX V

George Hathaway Goff Property at the time of his death in 1903

Home Farm, New Street with buildings, 160 acres	$ 6,000.00
George A. Case Lot	100.00
George Wheeler Lot	75.00
Hicks Fresh Meadows	50.00
Carpenter Lot, Rocky Hill	100.00
Carpenter Lot, Great Meadow Hill	50.00
Cushing Swamp	50.00
Hicks Swamp	60.00
Polly Goff Lot	20.00
Joanna Horton Lot	75.00
Harrie Williams Lot	15.00
Otis Nichols Lot	200.00
Nelson Baker Lot	40.00
Otis Peck Lot Squannakonk Swamp	100.00
Nelson Baker Swamp Lot	150.00
Rebecca Goff Lot	50.00
Nat Horton Lot	250.00
Simmons Lot	40.00
Talbot Horton Lot	100.00
Lot near A. F. Horton	100.00
One Half Ash Swamp Lot	50.00
Baylies Lot	150.00
D. M. White Lot	50.00
Pratt Lot, Norton, Massachusetts	100.00
Elephant Meadow	100.00
One Half Moulton Swamp Lot	122.00
Total	$ 8,197.00

PERSONAL PROPERTY

Cows	$1,000.00	Cider & barrels	$ 50.00
Bull	25.00	Potatoes	40.00
Horses	400.00	Turnips	22.00
Pigs	5.00	Corn	20.00
Oxen	200.00	Hay in two barns	475.00
Wagons	550.00	Sleds	50.00
Harnesses	100.00	Fertilizer	12.00
Farm tools	130.00	Hardwood Ties	200.00
Berry crates & boxes	25.00	Poles & post cut	
Tools in cellar	25.00	& wood	700.00
Charcoal Tools	12.00	Lumber	25.00
Pork	15.00	Charcoal	180.00
		Household furniture	400.00

Total	$4,661.00
Total Mortgages and Savings	$17,322.49
Total	$30,189.49

Source: George H. Goff Estate Probate 19484

APPENDIX VI

David W. Francis Property at the time of his death in 1913

REAL ESTATE
REHOBOTH

Homestead both sides of New Street	89 acres	$ 3,000.00
Senneca Bliss Lot, pasture and woodlot, New Street	7 acres	225.00
Henry I. Walker woodlot, Great Meadow Hill	45 acres	225.00
LaPlante woodlot	2 acres	10.00
H. A. Williams woodland	12 acres	125.00
Abbie A. Williams	5 acres	50.00
Betsey N. Cole	9.5 acres	50.00
One half Betsey Cole (undivided)	24 acres	125.00
R. Simmons woodlot	10 acres	200.00
Franklin Booth woodlot	5 acres	100.00
Henry A. Williams woodlot	22 acres	200.00
Betsey J. Hewitt woodlot	16 acres	75.00
Minerva Barney	6 acres	30.00
Deborah Goff	5 acres	200.00
Abbie Williams	5.5 acres	40.00
N. H. Horton	4.5 acres	25.00
N. H. Horton	2.5 acres	10.00
N. H. Horton	5 acres	60.00
John Moulton	6 acres	30.00
George S. Baker	3 acres	15.00
James M. Smith et al	3 acres	15.00
C. J. and N. Moulton	7 acres	25.00
G. and J. Moulton Lot 2	7 acres	7.00
Cora Crane and others	6 acres	50.00

Clarissa Francis	3 acres	20.00
One half Albert Goff	4 acres	10.00
One half Sam Peck	4 acres	10.00
Phillip Maker Lot	4 acres	125.00
Phillip Maker Lot	4 acres	125.00
Pine Lot	1 acre	40.00
Henry F. Horton and others	4 acres	20.00
Ferdinand Maker	2 acres	10.00

DIGHTON

Royal Peck Lot	13 acres	140.00
Bliss Lot on Winthrop Street	8.5 acres	500.00
George L. Goff	6.5 acres	110.00
One third undivided Josephine Briggs Lot	1 acre	2.00
One third Gideon Walker Lot	8 acres	8.00
A. J. Goff Lot	8 acres	80.00
Benjamin Goff Lot	6 acres	75.00
Tom Wetherell Lot	10.5 acres	100.00

TAUNTON

One half Chapman house		700.00
Two lots Agricultural Avenue		400.00
Totals	394.5 acres	$7,367.00

PERSONAL PROPERTY

7 Cows	$305.00	Express wagon	$ 5.00
3 Horses	235.00	Carryall	3.00
4 Pigs	50.00	3 Rolls paper	25.00
3 Sleds & pung	21.00	1 Top buggy	50.00
Roller & cart	40.00	1-2 Horse express wagon	50.00
Wheelbarrow	5.00		
Manure spreader	15.00	1 Democrat wagon	10.00
2 Horse rakes	15.00	Ploughs & Harrows	10.00
4-1 Horse farm wagons	90.00	Farming tools	3.00
1-2 Horse wagon	25.00	Chains & Whiffle trees	2.00
Wagon body & wheels	10.00	Platform scales	15.00
Mowing machines	5.00	Shingles	10.00
Open buggy	10.00	Plank outside	10.00

Pine lumber inside	$ 30.00	8 tons English hay	$ 128.00
Hardwood plank inside	5.00	Milk cans	10.00
Hay tedder	6.00	Household furniture	135.00
Cedar & chestnut posts	6.00	Potatoes	5.00
Harnesses	45.00		
		Total	1,389.00
Total Mortgages and Bank Accounts			17,794.00
		Total	26,550.00

Source: David W. Francis Estate Probate 33034

APPENDIX VII

Francis J. Wheeler Property at the time of his death on October 24, 1928

G.H. Goff lot 10 acres	$	100.00
Wheeler lot 15 acres		150.00
Harriet Gooding lot 10 acres		100.00
Nathan Horton lot 10 acres		75.00
R. Waterman lot 8 acres		40.00
Old Maids lot 3 acres		25.00
M. Westcott lot 8 acres		100.00
Home Farm and buildings less mortgages to amount of		1,600.00
Wood lot no. 1		15.00
Wood lot no. 2		15.00
Wood lot no. 3		20.00
Wood lot no. 4		40.00
Wood lot no. 5		125.00
Wood lot no. 6		75.00
Wood lot no. 7		150.00
Wood lot no. 8		150.00
Wood lot no. 9 Cole pasture		190.00
Wood lot no. 10		10.00
Wood lot no. 11		80.00
Wood lot no. 12		50.00
Wood lot no. 13		100.00
Wood lot no. 14		75.00
Wood lot no. 15		15.00
Wood lot no. 16		65.00
Wood lot no. 17		40.00
Wood lot no. 18		65.00
Wood lot no. 19		20.00
	Total	3,490.00

PERSONAL PROPERTY

1 Horse	$ 25.00	Lumber	$ 10.00
Harnesses	40.00	Chains	10.00
Hay	75.00	1 Democrat wagon	15.00
1 Buggy	15.00	1 covered express	
2 Sleds	15.00	wagon	35.00
1 Coal wagon	15.00	Sleigh	5.00
1 Express wagon	12.00	Wagon poles	5.00
Farm wagon	20.00	Ox yokes	5.00
1 Farm wagon	12.00	1 platform scale	5.00
Wheels and tongue		Weeder and tedder	2.00
for ox cart	10.00	Misc. farm tools	18.00
horse rake	10.00	15 hens $1.00 each	15.00
		Total	374.00
		Total	$ 3,864.00

Source: Francis J. Wheeler Estate Probate 58940

BIBLIOGRAPHY

Source	Abbreviation
1. Rehoboth Townsman A newspaper published weekly during the late 19th century	Townsman
2. Vital Records of Dighton By Louis H. Carr, 1983	Carr
3. Vital Records of Rehoboth By James Arnold, 1897	Arnold
4. Taunton Daily Gazette Taunton, Massachusetts	Gazette
5. History of Dighton By Helen Lane, 1962	Lane
6. History of Rehoboth By Rev. George H. Tilton, 1918	Tilton
7. In Old Rehoboth Edited by Sue Ellen Snape Rehoboth Historical Commission, 1979	In Old Rehoboth
8. Mighty Liberty Men By Sue Ellen Snape Rehoboth Revolutionary War Bicentennial Commission, 1976	MLM
9. Bristol County North Registry of Deeds Taunton, Massachusetts	Deed
10. Bristol County Registry of Probate Taunton, Massachusetts	Probate

NOTES

Cover Illustration

> The cover illustration is based on a photograph of the Henry W. Horton farm, circa 1900, shown on page 14 and the photograph of Henry W. Horton and his oxen on page 97.

Part I
Roy W. Horton, Farmer

CHAPTER I - The Paul Farm 1750-1850

Page:

3 James and Sarah Paul conveyed their house, farm, livestock and "one black boy's time" to their son Peter W. Paul in *Deed* 67/460 March 13, 1789.

4 Peter W. Paul's land division is described in *Probate* division 61/504 February 7, 1823; the widow's dower *Probate* 52/199 1816; and dower division *Probate* 56/33 June 1, 1819.

5 For the Wheeler Horton house location on Reservoir Avenue see *Deed* 108/118 May 27, 1820 Parcel 1 and 2, from his father Barnet (Barnard) Horton.

5 James Paul and his wife Betsey, James and his wife Eleanor are buried in the West Dighton Cemetery. James W. Paul's will is in *Probate* 182/272 May 3, 1859.

5 Benson Horton and his wife Pamela, Wheeler Horton and his wife Lucretia are buried in the West Dighton Cemetery.

5 For Barnet Horton's will see *Probate* 75/252 June 2, 1835.

5 For Wheeler Horton's property inventory and debts at the

time of his death see *Probate* 103/459 May 4, 1858 and 192/715.

6   The Genealogical Chart of the Horton and Paul family is based on information from the Vital Records of Rehoboth and Dighton, *Arnold* and *Carr,* and West Dighton Cemetery tombstone inscriptions.

7   In an interview on April 10, 1987, Roy W. Horton described how his grandfather James H. Horton was sent to live at the Paul farm as a young apprentice. In an article written in the *Gazette* on April 19, 1969 by Suzanne Withers Roy gave the second version that James did not arrive on the Paul farm until 1858.

8   James H. Horton advertised himself as a brick mason in the 1871 street atlas of Dighton.

8   James H. Horton's estate is in *Probate* 24689 and his obituary is in the *Gazette* April 4, 1907.

8   For a description of the lot conveyed to Charles Goff by James Paul see, *Deed*, 234/282 December 29, 1854.

9   The information about the two house fires and the rebuilding of the James H. Horton house was given in an interview with Arthur Morton, the present owner of the house.

9   The account of James H. Horton growing celery was in the *Townsman* November, 1881.

11 The Horton farm was conveyed to Henry W. Horton in *Deed* 537/436 July 24, 1896.

11 Gaius E. Horton purchased the Edson Place on Williams Street, Dighton in Deed 526/477 October 10, 1895.

CHAPTER II - Horton Farm 1860 - 1964

13 The vital records of the Henry W. Horton family from *Carr* and West Dighton Cemetery.

15 Death of James Harlan Horton from obituary in *Gazette* on December 19, 1910 and from an interview with Harlan Horton.

CHAPTER III - Farming in the Early 1900's

19   The list of suppliers to the Marble Dairy is from dairy records in the possession of Evelyn Marble Elting.

20   Letter from Weir Grammar School, *ibid.*

20   Marble Dairy operations from an interview with Evelyn Marble Elting.

25   The description of D. Lee Johnson picking up milk from farmers is from an interview with Ernest L. Horton, retired farmer, Wellington Street, Dighton.

31   An article on James H. Horton's hay fork in *Townsman* July 21, 1888.

35   The Bosworth Orchard is named after Elisha Bosworth who owned the Tinkham Farm in the early 1800's as per *Deeds* 95/196 1904 and 160/374 April 4, 1840.

36   The difficulty of blowing corn into the silo with bound corn stalks from an interview with Ernest L. Horton.

37   Selling the corn binder to Abbott Thayer from an interview with Harlan Horton.

38   Early history of the grist and sawmill at Perryville Rehoboth in *MLM* page 63 and *Tilton* page 271.

40   Roy going to wholesale market in Providence with horse and wagon from an article by Darrell Lambert in the *Gazette,* January 12, 1976.

43   Anecdote about Roy working on Dighton roads as a teenager from Elaine Varley, Dighton Historical Society.

44   The Horton farm house and its additions are described in Massachusetts Historical Commission Inventory by Stephen A. Cole September 5, 1976.

46   Excellent descriptions of the English and New England style barns and their evolution in *Big House, Little House, Back House and Barn* by Thomas C. Hubka in the New England Press.

48   The location of the Horton farm buildings from an inter-

view with Isabelle Horton Sears on November 15, 1991.

CHAPTER IV - Farm Animals

55 The description of how oxen were yoked and used on the farm originally described in an article in *In Old Rehoboth* by the author.

CHAPTER V - Schools

61 For the location of the old Fish School at the corner of Smith and Wellington Streets see *Deed* 243/386 February 26, 1834.

61 The New Fish School mentioned in *Lane* on page 217 and 219.

CHAPTER VI - Friends, Neighbors, Characters

73 The economics and methods of dairy farming in later years at the Horton farm from an interview with Harlan Horton.

77 The description of the Horton barn fire from an interview with Harlan Horton, Francis McClellan, and an article in the *Gazette* on May 6, 1964.

Part II
Roy Horton, Swamper

CHAPTER I - Swamps

86 For odd shaped lots in Manwhague Swamp, see Rehoboth Assessor's map 7, based on deed research by the author.

87 An article on the Anawan Club is in *Tilton* page 396.

88 Swamp lot names from deed research by the author.

CHAPTER II - Swamping

93 Cutting timber in the swamp from an article by Diana Alba in the *Gazette* November 8, 1976.

96 Roy cutting tall pine, *ibid.*

98 Squannakonk Swamp poem by Betsey D. Dyer first appeared as a slightly different version in the *Rehoboth Antiquarian Society 100th Anniversary* booklet in 1984.

CHAPTER IV - Elder Enoch Goff, Preacher

105 No sign of the first Goff church can now be seen at the corner of Cedar and Purchase Streets in Rehoboth. A large shed type building formerly known as the Lace Works now occupies the site.

107 A description of Elder Enoch Goff and his church is found in Massachusetts Historical Commission Inventory by Stephen A. Cole. Further description is given in articles in the *Spectator Newspaper* Somerset Massachusetts by Helen Lane on November 18, 1960, and in a *West Dighton Christian Church* booklet 1985 at the church office.

107 A description of the Elder Enoch Goff farm at the time of his death is in *Probate* 53/104 November 19, 1816.

107 According to Roy, his father built the present house at the end of Winfield Lane on the same foundation as the original Goff house.

113 Genealogical Chart based on *Probates, Carr* vital records, and West Dighton Cemetery tombstone inscriptions.

CHAPTER V - Wood Operators

118 A list of David W. Francis estate assets are listed in *Probate* 23064 January 14, 1906. (See appendix VI)

118 Examples of "Carpenter Gothic" house plans are given in *Architecture Is Elementary* by Nathan B. Winters published by Peregrine Smith Books, Salt Lake City on page 9.

119 A list of Frederick E. Francis' estate assets is given in *Probate* 23064 January 14, 1906. A funeral notice is given in the *Gazette* January 17, 1906.

120 Comments on David W. Francis, Jr. (Darby) from interviews with Pearl Wheeler Quint and Roy W. Horton.

122 Anecdotes about life of the Francis J. Wheeler farm from Pearl Wheeler Quint.

124 Map of the Francis J. Wheeler farm is based on a sketch drawn by Francis E. Wheeler, (1902-1986).

130 An article "Wheelers Corner" by the author is on page 16 in *In Old Rehoboth*.

135 A list of George Hathaway Goff's assets at the time of his death in *Probate* 19484 February 3, 1903. (See Appendix V.)

139 An account of the George Hathaway Goff accident in two *Gazette* articles: January 26, 1903 and January 30, 1903.

140 Taunton Teaming Company advertisement from *Taunton Directory* 1899.

140 Description of charcoal burning from an interview with Horace Smith.

141 Charcoal pits at the Ash Swamp from an interview with Walter Stott, Fairview Avenue, Rehoboth on October 30, 1958.

143 David W. Francis sold his Francis Street farm to Samuel E. Smith in *Deed* 613/31 October 2, 1906.

145 Anecdotes about life on the Smith farm from an interview with Horace Smith.

147 Cutting wood and hewing railroad ties from interviews with Horace Smith and Samuel S. Smith. See footnote in article "Wheelers Corner" by the author about cutting wood and ties on the hill in *In Old Rehoboth*.

150 Revolutionary War warning system in Rehoboth in *MLM* pages 62 and 92.

151 An account of H. P. Lovecraft's visit to Great Meadow Hill is in an article in the *Rehoboth Antiquarian Society 100th Anniversary* booklet entitled "Great Meadow Country Club," by the author.

152 John Smith killing the raccoon and the coon supper is in *Gazette* February, 1932.

Part III
Impressions and Reflections

CHAPTER II - The Swamps Today

163 Account of building the Horton barn from an interview with Ernest (Moe) Horton, Plain Street, Rehoboth on August 23, 1991.

CHAPTER III - Great Meadow Hill Today

172 Proposed Ski slope on Great Meadow Hill from conversations with author's family.

173 Lovecraft letter from *Selected Letters* of H. P. Lovecraft 1911-1924, Arkham House, Sauk City, Wisconsin.

CHAPTER IV - Roy W. Horton, Swamp Yankee

182 Articles on the Horton Memorial Wildlife Sanctuary in *Gazette* by Helen Lane on April 9, 1969 and in the Attleboro Sun by Suzanne Withers on April 19, 1969.

INDEX

A
Abigail Moulton Swamp 88
Alba, Diane viii
Anawan
  Club 87
  Indian Chief 84
  Inn 72
  School 70
  Street 25, 70, 140, 146, 166, 170
  Union Baptist Church 70
Araujo Farm 25
Armstrong, Robert 38
Arsenault,
  Jean 32
  Ted 32
Ash Swamp 85
Ash Swamp Lot 141
Assonet, MA 19
Attleboro, MA viii, 57, 75, 141, 146, 157

B
Bad Luck Pond 87
Bad Luck Swamp 83, 84, 85, 89, 102, 157
Baker Road 93
Baptist Church 105
Barrington, RI 150
Bay State Road 170
Belcher, Anthony 85
Bellanger Lot 94, 95, 159, 162, 175
Bellanger Swamp 88
Big Back Pasture 152, 170

Billings Road 145, 168
Bilodeau, Angela 108
Birch Hill
Birdsfoot Trefoil Hay 75
Bliss Swamp 88
Blackledge, Norma Wheeler vii
Block Island, RI 68
Boston Globe v
Boston, MA 40
Bosworth Orchard 35
Bowen,
  Harriet 174
  Maria 174
  Vashty 170, 173
Brazil's Package Store
  (Buffaloe's) 65
Breault Auto Sales 94
Briggs 112
Briggs,
  J. Emmons 19
  Pamela or Permilla 5
  Farm 19
Bristol County Agricultural
  School 77
Brockton, MA 13
Brook Street 84, 96, 101, 150
Buck's Hill 165
Burt Street 19, 33, 146
Butler Drive 152

C
California Lot Swamp 93
Camp Edwards 181
Camp Myles Standish 181
Canada 66, 123

Cape Cod 121
Cardoza Family 162
Carpenter,
  Christopher 162
  Col. Thomas 159
  Joseph, Jr viii
  Stephen 170
Carpenter Gothic 118
Carpenter Path 159
Carpenter Swamp 88
Carroll, Bethany Gaulin viii
Carswell,
  Larry viii
  Lydia (Dyer) viii
Case, George A 136
Case Orchard 35
Cavallaro, Vincent 85, 95, 127, 134
Cedar Street 19, 69, 84, 96, 105, 109, 163
Center Street 43
Chace,
  Albert 68, 69
  Andrew 93
  Barney 68, 69
  Ella 120
  Emeline 67, 68, 163
  Mary A 120
Chase, Priscilla viii
Chafee Farm 19
Chestnut Island 88, 160, 161
Chestnut Street 25, 150
Civil War 9, 86
Cold War 165
Commonwealth of Massachusetts 170
Coughlan, Frank 113, 161, 183
County Street 19, 59, 85, 88, 89, 116, 140, 157, 160, 161
Court Street 15
Crane, John 150
Cushing Swamp 136

Cutts, Nancy viii

D

Davis,
  John 143
  John II 170, 173
  Samuel 43
  Stephen H. 70, 71
Davis-Smith Hill
  Top Field 170
Dennen,
  Helen 162
  Richard 162
Devil's Pond 34, 35
Dexter, Maria Bowen 174
Dighton, MA ii, viii, 3, 5, 11, 21, 36, 40, 41, 43, 44, 48, 49, 59, 61, 62, 63, 65, 70, 73, 74, 75, 83, 92, 96, 101, 102, 105, 107, 109, 135, 137, 139, 140, 146, 147, 153, 157, 162, 175
  Fire Department 78
  Historical Society 43
  Poor Farm 25
  School 62, 91
Dighton-Berkley Bridge 67
Dighton Historical Society viii
Dighton-Rehoboth
  Regional High School i, vi, 66, 105
  School District 103
Drown, Karl 89
Duffy House 109
Dyer,
  Betsey Dexter viii, 43, 174
  E. Otis 39, 133, 179
  E. Otis, Jr viii, 112, 133, 162
  Justine viii
  Lydia viii

E

East Longmeadow, MA 103
East Providence, RI 40, 143, 151
Eastern Massachusetts Street
 Railway 20, 147
Easton, MA 75
Edson Place 11
Eisenhower, President 162
Elephant Meadow 136
Elting, Evelyn Holden viii, 22
Emerson, Ralph Waldo 81
Entwistle, Carol vii
Evans, Elsie 184

F

Fairview Avenue 43, 44, 70,
 141, 144, 146, 147, 151, 152,
 166, 168
Fall River, MA 86, 90, 157
Falmouth, MA ix
Fieldstone Drive iii, 32, 158
Figurado, John 66
Fine, Hyman 75
Fire Tower Road 146, 166, 168,
 171, 172, 173
Fish,
 Abner 61
 Daniel 61
 School 60, 61
Flibottes,
 Flossie 171
 Henry 171
Four Acre Lot 34, 35, 42
France 71
Francis,
 Bradford 119
 David W i, v, 69, 85, 102,
  103, 108, 114, 116, 118,
  125, 131, 135, 136, 143,
  150, 153, 158, 166, 177,
  182
 David Jr (Darby) 103, 119

Edward 129
Frederick Ernest v, 119, 122
Farm 134
Francis Street vii, 19, 122, 143,
 145, 147, 168, 171
Fuller, Nancy 70
Fuller's Island 160, 161

G

Genealogical Chart 6, 113
Goff 168
Goff,
 Andrew i
 Arthur v, viii, 135, 139, 140,
  142, 170
 Arthur H 70, 73, 116
 Benjamin i
 Charles 8
 Elder Meeting House 175
 Ellery L 86, 94, 159
 Emerson i, 117, 153
 Enoch i, ii, v, 102, 103, 105,
  109
 George Hathaway v, 62, 70,
  114, 116, 118, 125, 135,
  136, 138, 158, 170
 George M 166
 George N 131
 Harold A 125
 Isabelle 70
 Jesse 31
 Polly Lot 136
 Shubael 103, 108
 Baptismal Pool 112
 Farm 66, 71
 Hill 107
 Meeting House 73, 107
 Memorial Hall 131
 Swamp 88
Gonsalves,
 Everett 67, 163
 Tony 67
Goodings Hill 139

209

Gorham Street 84, 96
Great Britain
  Burford viii
  Northants viii
Great Meadow
  Country Club 151, 171
  Hill vii, 137, 143, 144, 145, 147, 150, 152, 153, 165, 166, 168, 170
  Carpenter Lot 136
Green Tree Lot 31
Grintry Lot iii, 31, 35
Gustafson Saw Mill 75

H

Hall,
  Abner 118
  Christopher viii
Hathaway Lot iii, 41, 42
Hicks Meadow 136
Hicks Swamp 136
Highway 895 157
Hill Field 143
Hingham Shipyard 181
History of
  Dighton iv
  Rehoboth iv
Holden,
  Evelyn viii
  George 84
  Warren 84
Holmes, Pamela viii, 52
Hornbine Road 67, 84, 163
Horton,
  Allie 53
  Andrew 7
  Barnet or Barnard 5, 112
  Benson 5, 112
  Charles 7
  Elsie ii, 108, 175
  Elwood v, 13, 25, 34, 62, 73, 94, 95, 142, 160, 161
  Ernest M viii, 25
  Ernest (Moe) 36, 84, 162, 163
  Everett 64, 65, 66
  Fair Building 59
  Gaius 8, 11, 17, 25, 101
  George H 89
  George L 89
  George R 13
  Hannah 9, 13, 73
  Harlan ii, v, vii, 15, 17, 29, 32, 53, 66, 73, 74, 75, 76, 77, 175
  Henry W ii, v, 8, 11, 13, 14, 25, 32, 36, 53, 54, 55, 67, 68, 73, 74, 86, 97, 102, 104, 105, 108, 109, 116, 142, 147, 162, 163
  Hot House Lot 48
  James H ii, 5, 7, 8, 9, 11, 13, 15, 31, 33, 40, 48, 49, 50, 66, 105, 112, 175
  Janice 182
  Jarvis 7
  Jennie 96
  Joanna Lot 136
  Lena May 8, 9
  Lindley 84, 96
  Lucretia 5
  Lyman 73, 161
  Mary A 11
  Mary E 8
  Nellie L 8
  Oren 7
  Pamela or Permilla (Briggs) 5
  Ralph 89
  Raymond ii, v, viii, 8, 13, 25, 32, 40, 44, 55, 62, 66, 73, 74, 77, 78, 79, 91, 104, 108, 119, 142, 180
  Roy Wheaton Horton (found throughout the book)
    Memorial Service 183
  Samuel 96

Swamp 88
Street 19, 64, 73, 102, 107, 158, 175
Thomas 8, 46, 79, 158
Wheeler 5
Wildlife Sanctuary 182

J

Jesse 66
Jesse Goff Lot 31
Jillson 92, 96
Jillson Sawmill 162
Johnson,
    D. Lee 25, 182
    Miriam viii
Jones,
    Elnathan 174
    Elnathan Lot 170

K

King Phillip's War 84
Kingman, Carol viii

L

Lane, Helen iv
Laneway Farm 19, 33
Leonard, Hannah J 13
Lincoln Dairy 26
Lindley Path 84, 162, 163
Little Compton, RI 184
Log Neck 84, 85, 86, 88, 162
Long Hill 5, 97, 166
Long Hill Lot 102
Long Stone 161
Lots
    Abigail Moulton Lot 175
    Ash Swamp Lot 141
    Bellanger Lot 94, 95, 159, 162, 175
    Elnathan Jones Lot 171
    Enoch Rounds Lot 172
    Four Acre Lot 34, 35, 42
    Great Meadow Carpenter Lot 136
    Green Tree Lot 31
    Grintry Lot iii, 31, 35
    Hathaway Lot iii, 41, 42
    Hot House Lot 48
    Jesse Goff Lot 31
    Joanna Horton Lot 136
    Joseph Nichols Lot 136
    Long Hill Lot 102
    Manchester Lot 67
    Moulton Lot 96, 102
    Orchard Lot 42, 125
    Peck Lot 171
    Polly Goff Lot 136
    Rock of Ages Lot 48
    Rocky Hill Carpenter Lot 136
    Rocky Lot 42
    Six Rod Way Lot 102
    Sprague Lot 88, 102
    Square Lot 31, 40, 42
    Thomas Witherell Lot 182
    Vashty Bowen Penno Lot 168, 171, 172
    Vineyard Lot 34
Lovecraft, Howard P 150, 171, 172, 173
Lunan,
    Joseph 86
    Joseph & Sons 164

M

Maine 87
Manchester Lot 67
Manwhague 96
Manwhague Cedar Swamp 67, 83, 84, 86, 87, 90, 162, 163, 164
Manwhague Farm 163
Maple Lane 59, 85, 88, 94, 95, 159, 160, 161, 162
Maple Street 19
Maple Swamp Road 66, 122, 125, 131, 135, 142

Marble,
   Charles C. Dairy viii, 19, 20, 21, 23, 25, 146
   Clifford 21
   Evelyn 22
   Palmer 21
Martin Swamp 88
Marvel,
   William Swamp 162
   Land 85
   Landing 160
Massachusetts 83, 157
Maxwell Swamp 88
McClellan,
   Francis viii, 41, 54, 76, 77, 78, 92, 161
   Janice viii
McCormick,
   Joseph 143
   Swamp 88
McKay, James 151
McNaly, Dorothy viii
McPherson, John viii
Merchant, Nathalie 85, 163
Miller Fertilizer Company 108
Ministerial Swamp 88, 90, 162
Minor, Milton 63
Morton,
   Arthur 10, 64
   Jane 10
Moulton,
   Abigail Lot 175
   George N 88, 101
   John B 88, 101
   Lot 96, 102
   Street 101
   Swamp 88
Muggleton, Paula viii
Munroe, Benjamin 25

N

Narragansett Bay 69, 85, 90
New England Power 34
New Street iv, viii, 19, 25, 62, 70, 73, 85, 94, 95, 102, 103, 108, 114, 115, 116, 118, 120, 122, 123, 126, 127, 132, 134, 135, 140, 142, 157, 162, 170
New York 74, 77
Newport, RI 150, 166
Nichols, Joseph Lot 136
Nike-Hercules Anti-Aircraft Missile Battery 165
Ninety-two Rod Swamp 88, 164
North Walker Street 26

O

Obar, Betsey (Dyer) viii
Oak Street 66, 64
Old Edson Place 11
Old Fields 125
Old Slough 34, 66
Olney and Paine Company 147, 153
Olson, Joseph 139
160 Rod Swamp 164
Orchard Lot 42, 125

P

Palmer River 143, 145, 151, 168
Paul,
   Caleb 3
   Farm 3, 13, 31, 35, 37, 40, 42, 73
   James 3, 44
   James Wheaton 5
   Job 3
   John 3
   Mary 7
   Peter White 3
   Sarah 3
Paul-Horton Farm 4, 47, 79, 158
Pavilion Farm 37
Pawtucket, RI 7, 115, 116, 117, 125, 147, 153
Peach Tree Orchard iii, 31, 35

Peck,
   Edmund 172, 174
   Harriet A. Bowen 174
   Lot 170, 174
   Street 145, 146, 147, 153, 170, 171
   Swamp 88
Pedo Baptist Church Ministerial Land 66
Penno, Vashty Bowen Lot 170, 171, 173
Perryville
   Grist Mill 38, 39, 48, 163
   Section 37, 125, 163
Perry's Corner 157
Phillips, Justine Dyer ix
Pierce, Wilson H 19
Pierce Hardware 15
Plain Street 84, 85, 96, 141, 163
Pleasant Street 101
Plymouth, MA 121
Pond Lilly Avenue 170
Poor Farm 41, 42
Portugal 66, 123
Providence, RI 7, 40, 62, 68, 69, 103 107, 115, 116, 157, 165, 166, 177, 183
Purchase Street 105, 109

Q

Quint, Pearl Wheeler vii, 70, 71, 123, 132

R

Rail Place 85, 163
Railway Line 130
Reed,
   Farm 19, 92
   George 162
Reed and Barton Silversmiths 141
Rego, John (Rabbitt) 162
Rehoboth, MA iv, vii, viii, 5, 37, 39, 44, 49, 59, 62, 67, 69, 70, 83, 88, 90, 94, 101, 102, 103, 105, 107, 108, 109, 114, 115, 116, 121, 122, 125, 126, 130, 132, 135, 137, 142, 143, 146, 147, 150, 152, 153, 157, 159, 62, 165, 168
   Congregational Church 88, 90
   Conservation Commission 164
   Fair 59
   Fire Department 78
   State Forest 171
   Village 86, 89, 94, 130
   Sanitary Landfill 163
Reservoir Avenue 5, 85, 102, 109, 158, 166
Rhode Island 83, 157
Rock of Ages Lot 48
Rocky Hill Carpenter Lot 136
Rocky Lot 42
Rocky Run Brook 96
Rodrigues 25
Roper, Ann viii, 52
Rose, Raymond 34
Rose Farm 19
Rounds,
   Enoch 168
   Enoch Lot 171
   Enos 170
Route 44 40, 62
Rumford, RI 63
Russell, Alexander 139

S

Salvas, Maxia 171
Saugus, MA 120
Schobel Farm 140
Seekonk, MA 70
Segregansett Country Club 130, 139
Segregansett Farm 19
Segregansett River 33, 92, 162
Sharp's Lot Road 93
Sheep River 143

Sheldon Lane 85
Short,
   Everett 145, 147, 171
   Hezekiah 170
Shube's (Shubael's) 66, 103
Sign Board Corner 84, 96
Simmons Street 19, 67, 68, 69, 85, 102, 109
Simons, Joseph 19
Simpson, John 57
Sisson, Julia 122
Six Rod Way Lot 102
Smith,
   Byron v, 143
   Carol vii
   Charles Swamp 162
   Elisha v, 143
   Emily 126
   Fairbanks 63
   Farm 19
   Fred M 82
   Horace E v, vii, 140, 141, 146, 150, 152, 153, 154
   John B v, 143, 151, 152
   Ruth 143
   Sam 165, 166, 168, 170, 171
   Samuel E v, 116, 143, 148, 149
   Samuel S v, 143, 145, 147, 151, 153, 158
   Street viii, 34, 41, 42, 61, 62, 67, 75, 158
Somerset, MA 120
Southern New England Bird Watchers 182
Sprague Lot 88, 102
Spring Hill Farm 19
Spring Street 84
Squannakonk
   Brook 87
   Cedar Swamp 83, 84, 85, 87
   Neck 85, 88
   Old Gangway 85
   Swamp viii, 59, 94, 95, 115, 123, 125, 157, 159, 160, 161, 162, 175
Square Lot 31, 40, 42
Stanley,
   Bertha 66
   John 66
Stiles and Hart Brick Company 141
Stony Path 84, 96, 163
Street Railway Company 130, 147
St. Valentine's Day Blizzard 95, 160
Swamps
   160 Rod Swamp 164
   Abigail Moulton Swamp 88
   Ash Swamp 85, 141
   Bad Luck Swamp 83, 84, 85, 89, 102, 157
   Bellanger Swamp 88
   Bliss Swamp 88
   California Lot Swamp 93
   Carpenter Swamp 88
   Cushing Swamp 136
   Great Cedar 82
   Goff Swamp 88
   Hicks Swamp 136
   Horton Swamp 88
   Manwhague Cedar Swamp 67, 83, 84, 86, 87, 90, 162, 163, 164
   Martin Swamp 88
   William Marvel Swamp 162
   Maxwell Swamp 88
   McCormick Swamp 88
   Ministerial Swamp 88, 90, 162
   Moulton Swamp 88
   Ninety-two Rod Swamp 88, 164
   Peck Swamp 88
   Seekonk Cedar 82
   Charles Smith Swamp 162
   Squannakonk

Cedar Swamp 83, 84, 85, 87
Swamp viii, 59, 94, 95, 115, 123, 125, 157, 159, 160, 161, 162, 175
Swamp Yankees 83
Swansea, MA 76, 93, 157
Syracuse, NY 119

T

Taunton, MA i, viii, 15, 26, 33, 37, 54, 55, 62, 63, 69, 71, 122, 125, 130, 134, 139, 141, 142, 147, 152, 157, 181
Taunton
  Avenue 70
  Daily Gazette 92
  High School 62, 103, 117, 135
  River iv, 90
  State Hospital 127
Taunton Teaming Company 139, 140
Taunton's 300th Anniversity 54
Thayer, Abbott 37
Thrasher's Landing 85
Tilton, George H iv
Tinkham
  Bessie 63
  Percy 32, 42, 63
  Farm viii, 32, 35, 78
Tremont Street 37
Tripp, Winsor 160
Trolley 147
Trolley Line 130
Tweedy,
  Bessie M. 63
  Howard 62, 63
  Talbot viii
26th Infantry Division Artillery 165

U

United States Government 165

V

Vandenberg Farm 19, 69
Varley,
  Christopher J 142
  Elaine viii
Vermont 73, 77
Vickery Point 85, 94, 95, 161
Vineyard Lot 34
Violette, Thomas 87

W

Wade Dairy 146
Wade's Corner 146
Walker, Charles 63
Walker Street 63
Washburn Hardware 15
Waterman,
  Jason 25
  Lester A 19, 25, 116, 140
  Ruth 170
Weeks, Sinclair 162
Weir School 20
Weir Street 55
Weld, William (Gov.) v
Wellington, VT 75
Wellington Street ii, iii, viii, 3, 9, 11, 19, 25, 36, 41, 42, 49, 59, 61, 67, 70, 73, 75, 78, 84, 95, 101, 104, 107, 109, 158, 177
West Dighton, MA iii, 64, 78, 83, 101, 107, 115
  Christian Congregational Church iv, 66, 69, 105
Westville Village 17, 54, 139
Wheeler,
  Edward v, 122, 123, 126, 127, 129, 131, 132, 134
  Elizabeth A. M. 120, 122
  Elkanah 122, 129, 134
  Farm 132
  Francis E vii
  Francis J v, vii, 69, 85, 94,

116, 120, 122, 124, 125,
126, 128, 131, 132, 133,
134, 136, 158, 162
George Lot 136
Henry v, 122, 123, 126, 129,
130, 132, 134, 152
Jasper 116, 122, 126, 127,
128, 130
Julia (Sisson) 126, 128, 132
Norma vii
Pearl 123, 130, 132
Royal i
Walter 129
Wheeler Homestead 134
Wheeler Street 122
Wheeler's Corner 25, 62, 117,
122, 131, 135, 147, 152
White, Robert 153
Williams Street viii, 11, 17, 19,
43, 59, 92, 96, 162
Wilson, Pres. Woodrow 71

Winfield Lane 44, 66, 107, 182
Winthrop Street (Route 44) 40,
62, 63, 64, 65, 70, 75, 85, 94,
116, 129, 130, 137, 139, 140,
141, 147, 160
Witherell,
Richard K. 64
Thomas Lot 182
Withers, Suzanne viii
Wolf's Den 66
World War I 71
World War II 181
Wyatt,
Bertram 21
Frederick 21

Z

Zuckerberg,
Leo 141
Muriel 141

ABOUT THE AUTHOR

E. Otis Dyer is an engineering graduate of the University of Maine. For 40 years he has conducted a land surveying and engineering business in Rehoboth.

Mr. Dyer is a 30 year member of the Rehoboth Historical Commission and President of the Rehoboth Antiquarian Society. He has written a number of articles on Rehoboth history and did the principal research for two historical books on Rehoboth published by the Town of Rehoboth and authored by Sue Ellen Snape, *Mighty Liberty Men* and *Rising From Cottages*.

The author, like many Rehoboth and Dighton residents today, is a direct descendant of Elder Enoch Goff and is also the 6th generation owner to farm the family homestead in Rehoboth, originally built in 1746 by Aaron Wheeler and bought in 1818 by Elder Goff's daughter Priscilla and her husband Stephen Bowen.

www.ingramcontent.com/pod-product-compliance
Lightning Source LLC
Chambersburg PA
CBHW062021220426
43662CB00010B/1417